Men-at-Arms • 543

German Troops in the American Revolution (2)

Hannover, Braunschweig, Hessen-Hanau, Waldeck, Ansbach-Bayreuth, and Anhalt-Zerbst

Robbie MacNiven • Illustrated by Marco Capparoni

Series editors Martin Windrow & Nick Reynolds

OSPREY PUBLISHING
Bloomsbury Publishing Plc
Kemp House, Chawley Park, Cumnor Hill, Oxford OX2 9PH, UK
29 Earlsfort Terrace, Dublin 2, Ireland
1385 Broadway, 5th Floor, New York, NY 10018, USA
E-mail: info@ospreypublishing.com
www.ospreypublishing.com

OSPREY is a trademark of Osprey Publishing Ltd

First published in Great Britain in 2025

© Osprey Publishing Ltd, 2025

ISBN: PB 9781472840196; eBook 9781472840202;
ePDF 9781472840172; XML 9781472840189

25 26 27 28 29   10 9 8 7 6 5 4 3 2 1

Index by Rob Munro
Typeset by PDQ Digital Media Solutions, Bungay, UK
Printed by Repro India Ltd.

Osprey Publishing supports the Woodland Trust, the UK's leading woodland conservation charity.

To find out more about our authors and books visit **www.ospreypublishing.com**. Here you will find extracts, author interviews, details of forthcoming events and the option to sign up for our newsletter.

Title-page photograph: Detail of the lock of a German musket captured at the battle of Bennington. While German troops sometimes used British muskets, most were equipped by their own state with weapons built at various German manufactories. This weapon is based on the models used by the Prussian Army of the period. Though popular histories claim muskets were entirely inaccurate over 100yd, many firefights during the American Revolutionary War took place at this range, or at even greater distances. (Lane Turner/The Boston Globe via Getty Images)

GERMAN TROOPS IN THE AMERICAN REVOLUTION (2)

HANNOVER, BRAUNSCHWEIG, HESSEN-HANAU, WALDECK, ANSBACH-BAYREUTH, AND ANHALT-ZERBST

INTRODUCTION

While unrest had been building in Britain's American colonies throughout the 1760s, the scale of the armed rebellion in 1775 at what marked the beginning of the American Revolutionary War (1775–83) still caught both King George III and the British parliament by surprise. It would take time to recruit and deploy sufficient numbers of fully trained soldiers to quash the revolution, time that Britain did not have. As an expedient, military planners turned to a solution that had served them well in the past – hiring soldiers from allied German states.

During the 18th century Germany was not yet a unified nation, and in order to keep their independence most of the plethora of states that constituted the region were required to maintain standing armies. This came with a heavy financial burden, and consequently the princes of German territories were happy to sign treaties with larger powers whereby they would provide military assistance in exchange for large financial reimbursements. In this way, each state was able to maintain its own army while relieving the financial burden of doing so, and its soldiers gained potentially valuable combat experience abroad.

Unidentified German troops in British service assemble before embarkation for North America. (Prisma/UIG/Getty Images)

This engraving by Franz Xavier Habermann (1721–96) depicts British and German troops in New York, September 1776. (MPI/Getty Images)

This spontoon brought to North America appears to bear the monogram of Frederick II of Prussia, whose formidable army was the model for many of the German states whose troops fought in the American Revolutionary War. (Met Museum/CC0/Gift of William H. Riggs, 1913)

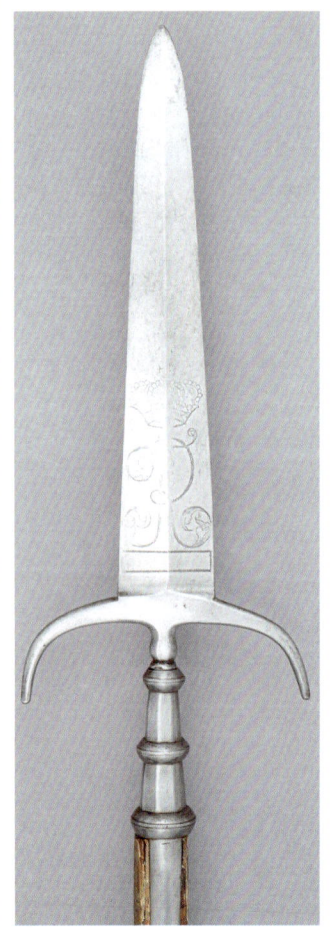

All of Europe's major powers hired what later became known as *Subsidientruppen*, or subsidy troops, from German states, though Britain was arguably their most consistent employer. This was partly due to the close links between Britain's monarchy and the German state of Hannover, and partly because the financial requirements of having a strong navy coupled with the public's distrust of a standing army meant Britain's own land forces tended to be limited in size.

It is therefore unsurprising that Britain sought to augment its manpower at the outbreak of the war by turning once more to the German states for aid. Britain was Hessen-Cassel's most regular client, and because that particular state provided the largest single armed contingent, "Hessian" became shorthand for any German troops hired by the British. In reality, however, only a little over one-half of the subsidy troops who fought during the war hailed from Hessen-Cassel or its neighbor, Hessen-Hanau. Five other states – Hannover, Braunschweig-Wolfenbüttel, Waldeck, Ansbach-Bayreuth, and Anhalt-Zerbst – also sent Britain military assistance by way of auxiliary corps.

Hannover was the first to do so, deploying five battalions of infantry to the Mediterranean in late 1775 and sending two more to India near the close of the war. British negotiators, particularly the British Army officer assigned to liaise with the authorities of the German states, Colonel William Faucitt (also Fawcett), worked to secure further aid. Braunschweig followed Hannover on January 9, 1776, signing a treaty that provided a corps of a little over 4,000 men, after Hessen-Cassel's the second-largest German contingent of the war. Hessen-Cassel signed on January 15, 1776, followed by its neighbor, Hessen-Hanau, on February 5, 1776, Waldeck on April 20, 1776, Ansbach-Bayreuth on February 1, 1777, and finally Anhalt-Zerbst in October 1777. In total, German states other than Hessen-Cassel provided around 15,000 troops for British service over the course of the American Revolutionary War, including light infantry, cavalry, and artillery, and played vital roles in campaigns such as Saratoga (September 19 and October 7, 1777) and the siege of Gibraltar (June 24, 1779–February 7, 1783). Without their involvement, Britain's war effort would have been significantly weakened.

HANNOVER

Britain's 1701 Act of Settlement specified that if King William III or his expected successor, the soon-to-be Queen Anne, failed to produce any heirs, the royal lineage would pass to Anne's second cousin, Sophia, *Kurfürstin* (Electress) of Hannover, thus ensuring the Protestant succession. Sophia died in May 1714, however, and Anne likewise passed away that August, ensuring that Sophia's son George Louis became George I of Great Britain and Ireland on August 1, 1714. While assuming his new duties as king of Britain, George did not give up his preexisting role as Elector of Hannover. The German state – itself part of the wider Holy Roman Empire – therefore became closely aligned with Great Britain.

Hanoverian soldiers were deployed to Britain in 1715 during the Jacobite rising in Scotland, and the War of the Austrian Succession (1740–48) saw large numbers of British and Hanoverian troops fighting side-by-side as part of the Pragmatic Army, for a while under the direct command of George II. During the Seven Years' War (1756–63), Hanoverian regiments again arrived in Britain to guard against the threat of a French landing in 1756. George II, fearing that Hannover would itself be invaded by France, formed an alliance with Frederick II of Prussia, widening the scope of the conflict. The French did indeed attack Hannover in 1757, occupying it briefly after their victory at the battle of Hastenbeck (July 26, 1757). The French forces were, however, compelled to withdraw the next year. Hanoverian and British troops continued to serve together with the Army of Observation in the European theater for the duration of the Seven Years' War.

Much like Hessen-Cassel, Hannover thus had a history of close military relations with Britain prior to the commencement of the American Revolutionary War. This made it a prime candidate when, in 1775, Britain realized that manpower shortages would force it to look for foreign assistance in suppressing the rebelling American colonies. Some Members of Parliament requested that George III use his influence as the Elector of Hannover to requisition reinforcements. This was a politically risky maneuver, however, as Parliament as a whole had not approved the use of what detractors called foreign mercenaries, and some sections of public opinion were firmly against the idea of sending German soldiers to fight British subjects, even if those subjects were in open rebellion.

Regardless of this, George III wrote to Field Marshal August Friedrich von Spörcken, the commander of the Hanoverian Army and a Seven Years' War veteran, and worked out a contribution toward the British war effort.

Hanoverian Major-General August de la Motte. A Seven Years' War veteran, de la Motte served during the siege of Gibraltar, initially as a colonel in command of the three Hanoverian battalions that formed a vital part of the garrison. (The History Collection/Alamy Stock Photo)

Organization and deployment

At the outbreak of the American Revolutionary War, a standard Hanoverian line-infantry regiment consisted of two battalions, each of six companies. Five of these were musketeer companies each composed of 75 officers and men, while the sixth was a larger grenadier company of 85 officers and men. With an additional staff of 13 officers and noncommissioned officers, a single battalion consisted on paper of 473 officers and men. Two women were also allowed on the official establishment.

Unlike the British Army, Hanoverian regiments were still identified by the name of their *Inhaber* (colonel-in-chief) rather than using a numerical sequence, though numbers were introduced in 1783. This could potentially cause some confusion when the colonel-in-chief changed, thereby technically changing the name of a regiment, potentially mid-campaign. Further complexity was added by the fact that there were three levels of senior regimental officer, with the colonel-in-chief at the pinnacle, followed by a commander, and then lastly a field commander (usually a lieutenant-colonel, or major), this last being the individual who actually traveled with the regiment on campaign and oversaw its day-to-day business both in and out of action.

The British plan for the Hanoverian regiments was to use them as garrison troops for the strategic Mediterranean holdings of Gibraltar and Minorca. A number of the British infantry regiments stationed there could then be freed for use further overseas, including in North America, the Caribbean, and India. In 1775 the British 1st, 2nd, and 69th regiments of Foot were instructed to return to Britain from Gibraltar, while part of the Minorca garrison consisting of the 13th and 25th regiments of Foot were to do likewise. Five Hanoverian battalions – one each from five separate regiments – were assigned to be their replacements, three for Gibraltar and two for Minorca (Dornfest 1983: 58).

The first battalion of the Gibraltar Brigade was the 1st Battalion, Infanterie-Regiment von Reden (later the 3. Infanterie-Regiment). Lieutenant-General Johann Wilhelm von Reden was the colonel-in-chief and Colonel Ernst Wilhelm von Friesenhausen was the commander. The field commander was Lieutenant-Colonel Johann Gottfried von Walthausen until his death by drowning on November 13, 1775, and subsequently Lieutenant-Colonel Gustav Friedrich von Dachenhausen.

The second battalion of the Gibraltar Brigade was the 1st Battalion, Infanterie-Regiment de la Motte (later the 5. Infanterie-Regiment). Colonel August de la Motte was the colonel-in-chief and also the commander, while Major Bernhard Wilhelm von Schlepegrell was the field commander.

The third battalion of the Gibraltar Brigade was the 1st Battalion, Infanterie-Regiment von Hardenberg (later the 6. Infanterie-Regiment). Field Marshal Christian Ludwig von Hardenberg was the colonel-in-chief until his death on 26 November 1781, when he was succeeded by Major-General Heinrich Bernhard von Sydow. Lieutenant-Colonel Georg Wilhelm von dem Bussche was both the commander and also the field commander until he returned to Hannover in 1776, being replaced as field commander by Lieutenant-Colonel Ernst August von Hugo.

The first battalion of the Minorca Brigade was the 2nd Battalion, Infanterie-Regiment Prinz Ernst (later the 8. Infanterie-Regiment). Major-General Ernst Gottlob Albrecht, Duke of Mecklenburg, was the colonel-in-chief, while Lieutenant-Colonel Johann Wilhelm von Linsing was both the commander and the field commander.

The second battalion of the Minorca Brigade was the 2nd Battalion, Infanterie-Regiment von Goldacker (later the 11. Infanterie-Regiment). Major-General Burchard Rudolph von Goldacker was the colonel-in-chief, while Colonel Heinrich Bernhard von Sydow was both the commander and the field commander until his promotion to major-general in 1778, at which time Major Friedrich Christian von Hager replaced him as field commander.

While the Hanoverian service in the Mediterranean is the best-known element of their contribution toward the British war effort during the American Revolutionary War, it was not the only one. Owing to increasing pressures in India, the East India Company successfully petitioned an initially reluctant George III to use his position as Elector of Hannover to have reinforcements sent from Germany. The king gave instructions to the Minister for Electorate Affairs, Johann Friedrich Karl von Alvensleben, to raise a new Hanoverian regiment for service in India. It was to consist of two battalions, each made up of one grenadier, one light, and eight fusilier companies. Each company was to consist of one captain, two lieutenants, one ensign, three sergeants, one clerk,

The Siege of Gibraltar, 1782 by George Carter (1734–94). During the siege Hanoverian officers played senior roles in the defense of the fortress. Promoted from colonel to major-general and then lieutenant-general, the Hanoverian August de la Motte served as third-in-command of the entire garrison. (Art Collection 2/Alamy Stock Photo)

four corporals, two drummers, 12 lance-corporals, and 74 privates. The regimental staff consisted of one lieutenant-colonel, one major, one captain-lieutenant (commanding the colonel's company), one adjutant-major, one adjutant, one judge, one chaplain, one surgeon, two cadets, five surgeon's mates, one drum-major, four musicians, one armorer, and one provost. The force would also include two cannon per battalion, operated by an additional sergeant, two corporals, and 12 gunners per piece (Decurion 1937: 206).

The agreement between Hannover and the East India Company was signed on September 7, 1781. Initially, the regiment was set to serve the company for seven years, and though its recruits were to be drawn from Hannover and the neighboring states, it was stipulated that foreigners were to be the primary focus of the recruiting drive. Despite this, the final makeup of the regiment was a largely even split between men from Hannover and those from elsewhere.

Not long before departing to India, the force was reorganized from one regiment of two battalions to two regiments of one battalion each. Unlike other Hanoverian infantry regiments in 1781, these were given numerical designations, 15 and 16, but when the rest of the Army adopted a numbered system in 1783 they were redesignated as the 14. and 15. Infanterie-Regimenter. Unlike the battalions serving at Gibraltar and Minorca, both of the regiments sent to India combined the roles of colonel-in-chief, commander, and field commander in one person: the 15. Infanterie-Regiment was commanded by Colonel Carl Ludwig Reinbold and the 16. Infanterie-Regiment by Lieutenant-Colonel August von Wangenheim.

Service history

The fortunes of the Hanoverian regiments during the American Revolutionary War were mixed. The Gibraltar garrison became embroiled in the longest siege in British history when a Franco-Spanish force invested Gibraltar by both land and sea in June 1779. The Hanoverian troops served well, and the senior Hanoverian officer, Colonel de la Motte, also acted as third-in-command of the entire garrison. The Franco-Spanish efforts were eventually defeated and the siege lifted in February 1783. The three Hanoverian regiments returned home in September 1784 to public acclaim. "Gibraltar" was awarded to them as a battle honor, and the name continued to be worn on uniform cuffs by their antecedent regiments in the Imperial German Army through to World War I.

The Minorca garrison's fate was less illustrious. Like Gibraltar, the island was attacked by a Franco-Spanish force, this time in August 1781. The British and Hanoverian defenders concentrated at St. Philip's Castle, which held out again multiple assaults and a powerful bombardment for five months before surrendering. The Prinz Ernst and von Goldacker regiments marched into captivity, and were released at the end of the war. They performed garrison duties in Plymouth before returning home in June 1784.

The regiments deployed to India spent the longest length of time in British service. They sailed in several detachments to Madras, arriving in time to see combat during the Second Anglo-Mysore War (1780–84). They were present at a number of engagements, including the siege of Cuddalore (June–July 1783), where they served well but suffered significant casualties. News of a preliminary peace ended the siege, and the Hanoverians continued to serve the East India Company in minor conflicts for the rest of the decade. The 15. Infanterie-Regiment (formerly numbered 16) eventually returned home in 1791 and the 14. Infanterie-Regiment (formerly numbered 15) in 1792. When including reinforcements sent intermittently from Hannover, it is estimated that around 3,000 Hanoverians served in India over this period (Dornfest 1983: 61).

Uniforms and personal equipment

Hanoverian infantry uniforms were very similar to British ones, most notably in the use of what became known as madder red for the coloration of the enlisted men's coats and scarlet for the officers. Like the British, the Hanoverians also used facing colors to differentiate between regiments, but some also used the coloration of shoulder straps. Hanoverian officers wore yellow waist sashes, rather than the crimson ones used by the British, and silver lace in line-infantry regiments, gold lace being reserved for officers of the Garde-Regiment. The battalions serving at Gibraltar and Minorca were marked by the following distinctions: von Reden, black facings, white vest and breeches, white shoulder straps; de la Motte, lemon-yellow facings, white vest and breeches, red shoulder straps; von Hardenberg/von Sydow, straw facings, vest, breeches, and shoulder straps; Prinz Ernst, white facings, vest, and breeches, red shoulder straps; von Goldacker, black facings, straw vest and breeches, red shoulder straps.

Colonel H.A. de Scheiter suggested the following uniform, arms, and equipment for the Hanoverian force to be sent to India in 1781, which was approved by the king. Each man would receive one scarlet coat with green facings, its lining straw-colored, with yellow buttons, the sergeant's of fine cloth with a sash. After the regiment of two battalions was split into two regiments of one battalion each, slight adjustments were made to differentiate them by giving the 15. Infanterie-Regiment green shoulder straps, and the 16. Infanterie-Regiment red shoulder straps. The uniform coat was accompanied by one vest and white breeches of the same cloth; one pair of linen trousers and black half spatterdashes; one pair of worsted stockings, shoes, and black, full-length gaiters. Each man also received a black stock and a string for tying the hair. Equipment included a leather haversack, a belt with a saber, a belt for a cartridge box, a musket and a bayonet. Each noncommissioned officer would also receive a halberd and the grenadiers fur caps, and the whole regiment would have four pairs of colors and 40 camp colors (Decurion 1937: 206).

The weaponry issued to the Hanoverian regiments was manufactured at the Königliche Gewehrfabrik at Herzberg am Harz (Moller 2011a: 419). Hanoverian muskets such as the Modell 1766 or 1767 differed by the style of the lock plates and variation in the ramrods, which were changed to a cylindrical-headed pattern in 1778. Barrels were marked with a fir-tree motif, the mark of the Hanoverian inspector Gottfried Sigismund Tanner. The locks of Hanoverian muskets were engraved with the "GR" cipher of George III in his role as Elector of Hannover, with the same symbol repeated on Hanoverian polearms and colors (Moller 2011a: 14–15).

Though this 1793 artwork of a Hanoverian officer postdates the American Revolutionary War, it shows the influence British uniforms had on the Hanoverian military. (Anne S.K. Brown Military Collection, Brown University Library)

Painted by Anna Rosina de Gasc (1713–83), this portrait of the ruler of Braunschweig-Wolfenbüttel, Duke Karl I, dates from 1779. The relatively unostentatious uniform gives an indication of the cut and style of Braunschweig uniforms, with its lack of lace and split-sided cuffs. (The History Collection/Alamy Stock Photo)

BRAUNSCHWEIG-WOLFENBÜTTEL

With a population of approximately 150,000 during the revolutionary period, the Duchy of Braunschweig-Wolfenbüttel – distinct from Braunschweig-Lüneburg, also known as Hannover – possessed close ties to the British monarchy. The duchy's heir, Karl Wilhelm Ferdinand, was married to King George III's sister, Princess Augusta Frederica, while neighboring Hannover was ruled by George in his role as that state's elector. These ties combined with the duchy's heavy debts meant Braunschweig-Wolfenbüttel was the first German state after Hannover to sign a military agreement with Britain. A treaty was ratified on January 9, 1776, whereby Braunschweig would send a corps consisting of four line-infantry regiments, one grenadier battalion, one dragoon regiment, and one light battalion – including a *Jäger* company – for service with the British, a total of over 4,000 men. After Hessen-Cassel, Braunschweig-Wolfenbüttel therefore provided the most troops to the British crown over the course of the American Revolutionary War.

Organization and deployment

In 1776 the two Braunschweig line-infantry regiments, Prinz Friedrich and von Rhetz, each had their two battalions reorganized into four single-battalion regiments. The first battalions of Prinz Friedrich and von Rhetz remained, while the former second battalion of Prinz Friedrich became the Infanterie-Regiment Riedesel, and the former second battalion of von Rhetz became Infanterie-Regiment Specht. The grenadier companies from each of these four regiments were detached to form a composite grenadier battalion, von Breymann, consisting of four companies.

On paper, each of the four infantry regiments had five musketeer companies, each consisting of four officers, five sergeants, seven corporals, 105 privates, and three drummers, along with four officers' servants, a surgeon, and a clerk. There was also a regimental staff of seven officers and 18 other ranks.

Lieutenant-General Prinz Friedrich August was the colonel-in-chief of Infanterie-Regiment Prinz Friedrich; the commander was Major-General Eckhard Heinrich von Stammer, while the field commander was Lieutenant-Colonel Christian J. Prätorius.

Major-General Friedrich Adolf Riedesel was the colonel-in-chief of Infanterie-Regiment Riedesel, while Lieutenant-Colonel Ernst Ludwig Wilhelm von Speth was both the commander and the field commander.

Colonel Johann Friedrich Specht was the colonel-in-chief of Infanterie-Regiment Specht, while Major Carl Friedrich von Ehrenkrook was both the commander and the field commander.

Major-General August Wilhelm von Rhetz was the colonel-in-chief of Infanterie-Regiment von Rhetz; the unit's field commander was Lieutenant-Colonel Johann Gustav von Ehrenkrook, though he remained in Canada during Major-General John Burgoyne's 1777 campaign along the Hudson River, during which the regiment was commanded in combat by Major Balthasar Bogislaus von Lucke.

Grenadier-Bataillon von Breymann's four companies each consisted of four officers and 135 other ranks, plus a battalion staff of three officers and five other ranks, for a combined battalion strength of 19 officers and 545 other ranks. The unit was commanded by Lieutenant-Colonel

Heinrich von Breymann until his death at the battle of Bemis Heights (October 7, 1777), whereupon it was led by Major (later Lieutenant-Colonel) Otto C.A. von Mengen.

The one Braunschweig-Wolfenbüttel cavalry regiment sent to North America, Dragoner-Regiment Prinz Ludwig, consisted on paper of a staff of eight officers and 16 other ranks overseeing four troops, each consisting of three officers and 75 enlisted men and noncommissioned officers, giving a total regimental strength of 20 officers and 316 other ranks. The regiment sailed to North America without horses, expecting to be assigned or to collect mounts upon arriving in Canada, but there were never enough for the whole regiment to be mounted. Prinz Ludwig Ernst was the regiment's colonel-in-chief; its commander was Colonel Friedrich Adolf Riedesel, while its field commander was Lieutenant-Colonel Friedrich Baum until his death on August 18, 1777, two days after the battle of Bennington, and thereafter Major J.C. von Meibom.

It should be noted that besides Riedesel, none of the colonels-in-chief mentioned above served in North America (Haarmann 1970: 140–43).

The final Braunschweig-Wolfenbüttel unit sent to North America in 1776 was Leichtes Infanterie-Bataillon von Barner. Commanded by Major Ferdinand Albrecht von Barner, it consisted of one *Jäger* company of four officers and 143 other ranks, and four light-infantry companies each of four officers and 121 other ranks. Along with a battalion staff of four officers and seven other ranks, the battalion had a combined total of 24 officers and 634 other ranks. It seems as though the purpose of the four light-infantry companies was to provide formed support, with muskets and bayonets, for the *Jäger* company to operate alongside and fall back on, rather than fighting in a purely light-infantry capacity, as composite British light-infantry battalions tended to do.

Before setting out from their homeland in early 1776, the Braunschweig contingent was divided into two divisions, both totaling around 2,000 men. The first, slightly larger division left on February 22, 1776, marching roughly 100 miles to Stade near the mouth of the Elbe River, which they reached on March 5. There, under the directions of Colonel William Faucitt, they took their new oath of allegiance and embarked on transports, setting sail for Britain on March 18. They arrived at Portsmouth on March 28, joining a larger British fleet – including the Hessen-Hanau corps – which departed on April 3, and arrived in Québec on June 1. The second Braunschweig division followed the first in late May 1776.

In 1778, a new Braunschweig infantry regiment, von Ehrenkrook, was created under the command of Lieutenant-Colonel Johann Gustav von Ehrenkrook. It was an ad hoc formation composed of one battalion manned by invalids and detachments that had avoided the defeat of the majority of the Braunschweig corps during the Saratoga campaign, as well as escapees and exchanged prisoners, alongside Leichtes Infanterie-Bataillon von Barner, which had not been present at Saratoga.

Service history

Commanded by Major-General Friedrich Adolf Riedesel, the Braunschweig regiments were initially employed in mopping up revolutionary forces in the wake of the Patriots' failed invasion of Canada in late 1775. From June 7, 1776, not long after arriving at Québec on June 1, Riedesel led Grenadier-Bataillon von Breymann and detachments of British, Loyalist, Native American, and Hessen-Hanau troops along the south bank of the St. Lawrence River in order to relieve Montréal.

RIGHT
Unlike the other Braunschweig infantry regiments, Infanterie-Regiment Prinz Friedrich was considered a "garrison regiment," a lower-quality unit that was tasked with defending Fort Ticonderoga after it was taken by Crown Forces. This ensured the regiment avoided the defeat at Saratoga. (Staatsarchiv Braunschweig H VI 6 Nr. 27)

FAR RIGHT
A musketeer of Infanterie-Regiment Riedesel. Formed initially from the second battalion of Infanterie-Regiment Prinz Friedrich, Infanterie-Regiment Riedesel was nominally led by the commander of the Braunschweig detachment, but in the field was under the orders of Lieutenant-Colonel Ernst von Speth. (Staatsarchiv Braunschweig H VI 6 Nr. 27)

The Braunschweig regiments played an important role in Burgoyne's campaign of 1777. Beforehand, Riedesel noted with apparent dissatisfaction that the British were asking him to adopt a number of the tactical changes they had already implemented for fighting in North America. In a letter to the Duke of Braunschweig, Riedesel wrote about what he called the French method of forming lines at open or extended order, and mentioned teaching his troops how to operate in wooded terrain (Eelkin 1893: 271). Unlike the commanders of a number of other German states, notably Hessen-Cassel, Riedesel was permitted by his ruler to introduce tactical changes to address the difficulties of fighting in North America.

Riedesel seems to have had some success in implementing these changes prior to the commencement of the 1777 campaign. In his journal he describes the loose, rapid method of fire and maneuver adopted by his Braunschweig troops:

> As soon as the first line has jumped into the supposed ditch, the command 'fire' is given, when the first line fires, reloads its guns, gets up out of the ditch, and hides behind a tree, rock, shrub or whatever is at hand, at the same time firing off four cartridges in such a manner that the line is kept as straight as possible. As soon as the first line has fired off the four cartridges, the second line advances and fires off the same number in the same manner. While this is taking place, the woods have been thoroughly ransacked by the sharp shooters who have thus become familiar with every part of it. (Quoted in Eelkin 1868: 64)

ABOVE LEFT
A grenadier of Infanterie-Regiment Prinz Friedrich. The collar and cuffs are colored red, seemingly in error. (Anne S.K. Brown Military Collection, Brown University Library)

ABOVE RIGHT
A grenadier of Infanterie-Regiment Riedesel. Again, the facing are red, rather than the yellow normally associated with this unit. (Anne S.K. Brown Military Collection, Brown University Library)

In a general order to the Braunschweig corps on August 26, 1777, Riedesel reiterated the importance of using cover and dispersed methods of fighting in wooded terrain, juxtaposed with the more traditional close-order drill in two or three ranks in the open.

Part of the Braunschweig corps was engaged at the battle of Hubbardton (July 7, 1777), and at Bennington. At the latter, most of the Dragoner-Regiment Prinz Ludwig was lost, and its commander, Lieutenant-Colonel Friederich Baum, was mortally wounded. At the battle of Freeman's Farm (September 19, 1777), Riedesel's forces, ordered to guard the baggage train, advanced into action in time to save Burgoyne's main body. A few weeks later, on October 7, the battle of Bemis Height – the decisive action of the Saratoga campaign – closed with the rebels' capture of a redoubt held by Grenadier-Bataillon von Breymann. Seemingly, Breymann was killed by his own men when he began lashing out at them with his sword in response to their perceived cowardice.

With defeat at Saratoga, most of the Braunschweig corps marched into captivity as part of the so-called Convention Army. Riedesel was transferred as part of a prisoner exchange in time to command troops again in New York and then Canada before the end of the American Revolutionary War, though he did not see action. Some elements of the Braunschweig corps had avoided the Saratoga disaster, namely Infanterie-Regiment Prinz Friedrich, which had been left behind to garrison Fort Ticonderoga, and most of Leichtes Infanterie-Bataillon von Barner, which was incorporated into the new Infanterie-Regiment von Ehrenkrook. None of these, however, saw significant action during the rest of the war.

At the end of the conflict, the Duke of Braunschweig encouraged those who wished to leave his army and remain living in North America to do so, an act that would aid his own demobilization efforts and remove the financial and social burden of soldiers returning home.

Uniforms and personal equipment

All Braunschweig infantrymen, bar the *Jäger* of Leichtes Infanterie-Bataillon von Barner who wore green, wore dark-blue Prussian-style

Two views of a cap belonging to a grenadier of Infanterie-Regiment Specht. The brass-plated front bears the Braunschweig cipher and the crest of a running horse. (Military and Historical Images Bank)

regimental coats with red lining; only musicians wore lace. The coat had a single shoulder strap on the wearer's left, set behind the shoulder, to support the cartridge-box belt. Musketeers and light infantrymen wore a white-laced cocked hat with unit-specific cords and a tassel and pompon, while the *Jäger* wore an unlaced cocked hat and the grenadiers a metal-fronted miter. Vests and breeches were white, the latter worn with knee-high black gaiters. It should be noted that in 1777, much of the Braunschweig corps – except the dragoons and *Jäger* – replaced their breeches and gaiters with gaitered trousers, mostly made from old sailcloth and British tents, some of which were striped. It should also be noted that, contrary to popular myths, the Braunschweig dragoons did not attempt to wear their heavy riding boots while serving as infantry.

Braunschweig officers were distinguished by silver- and gold-striped waist sashes, hat lace that was silver or gold depending on the color of the particular regimental buttons (silver matching with pewter or "white" buttons and gold with brass or "yellow" buttons), as well as gorgets bearing the running white horse insignia of Braunschweig. Turning to NCOs, Braunschweig infantry sergeants likewise had distinguishing silver- or gold-laced hats, black-and-white hat cords and pompoms, and carried a cane – used for corporal punishment – hooked over the second-from-top button on the right of the coat's front. Corporals were signified by white lace around their cuff buttons.

In terms of regimental distinctions, Infanterie-Regiment Prinz Friedrich's coats had yellow collars and cuffs, but were without lapels.

Eight white buttons were evenly spaced down either side of the coat's front, with two more on each cuff. Cocked hats had yellow-and-white cords and a tassel and pompom, which was yellow with a circular white center. Musicians wore yellow coats with light-blue facings and red lining. Drummers' coats were trimmed with white and yellow lace, while the drum-major and hautboys had silver lace on their hats.

Infanterie-Regiment Riedesel wore yellow facings. Buttons were white and those on the coat's lapels were spaced in a sequence of 1-2-1 on both sides, plus two buttons on each cuff. Cocked hats had yellow-and-white cords, and a yellow-and-white pompom. Musicians wore yellow coats with light-blue facings and red lining. Hautboys had silver lace on their cocked hats, and drummers' coats were trimmed with white and yellow lace.

Infanterie-Regiment Specht wore red facings. Buttons were yellow, and those on the coat's lapels were spaced in a sequence of 1-2-1 on both sides, plus two buttons on each cuff. Cocked hats had red-and-white cords and a red-and-white pompom. Musicians wore yellow coats with red facings and red lining. Drummers' coats were trimmed with lace, color unspecified, though it was probably white, along with 26 tassels.

Infanterie-Regiment von Rhetz wore white facings. Buttons were yellow, and those on the coat's lapels were spaced in a sequence of 1-2-1 on both sides, plus two buttons on each cuff. Cocked hats had red cords and a red pompom. Musicians wore yellow coats with white facings and red lining. The drum-major and hautboys' coats had silver lace and 26 tassels, the drummers similarly attired but likely less expensively.

RIGHT
A musketeer of Leichtes Infanterie-Bataillon von Barner. The musketeers of this unit were equipped like regular Braunschweig infantry, with smoothbore muskets and bayonets. Their purpose was to provide close support for the riflemen who, due to their slow-loading weapons, were vulnerable to sudden enemy assaults. (Staatsarchiv Braunschweig H VI 6 Nr. 27)

FAR RIGHT
A Braunschweig *Jäger*. While theoretically part of Leichtes Infanterie-Bataillon von Barner, the Braunschweig *Jäger* company, commanded by Captain Carl Geisau, often operated separately and on its own initiative. (Staatsarchiv Braunschweig H VI 6 Nr. 27)

The uniforms of Grenadier-Bataillon von Breymann mirrored those of whichever parent regiment each grenadier company had come from. Grenadier headwear consisted of a tall Prussian-style cap with a metal-plate front, cloth backing, and wool pompom. The color of the cloth backing matched the regimental facing colors, the metal plate matched the buttons (white or yellow), and the pompom matched those sported by the musketeer companies of the regiment. White piping decorated the cloth backing, apart from the von Rhetz company, whose facings (and thus cap backing) were white – their piping was red.

Leichtes Infanterie-Bataillon von Barner's *Jäger* wore green coats with red facings and green lining. Buttons were white, and those on the coat's lapels were spaced in a sequence of 1-2-1 on each side. Vests were green and breeches were buff, the latter worn with knee-high gray gaiters. Cocked hats were unlaced and had a green cockade. The musketeers of the battalion wore dark-blue Prussian-style coats like the other regiments, with black collars and cuffs but no lapels, and red lining. There were

ABOVE LEFT
Braunschweig *Jäger.* Note that his green uniform seems almost brown – one British commentator described how green coats put on in the spring would fade to brown with the autumn. (Anne S.K. Brown Military Collection, Brown University Library)

ABOVE RIGHT
A soldier of the Braunschweig artillery. (Anne S.K. Brown Military Collection, Brown University Library)

Duke Karl II was the ruler of Braunschweig-Wolfenbüttel after his father's death on March 26, 1780. Karl II and his father permitted their troops more tactical leeway than the forces of Hessen-Cassel. (Anne S.K. Brown Military Collection, Brown University Library)

A spontoon carried by a Braunschweig officer, bearing the cipher of the ruler, Duke Karl I. Beneath it are the words *NUNQUAM RETRORSUM*, "never backward," the motto of the Hanoverian Order of St. George, of which the ruler of Braunschweig-Wolfenbüttel was a member. (INTERFOTO/Alamy Stock Photo)

eight evenly spaced yellow buttons on each side of the coat's front, plus two buttons on each cuff. The drummers wore yellow coats with black facings and red lining, plus white, black, and yellow mixed lace – the drum-major also had gold lace along with his white, black, and yellow mixed lace.

Dragoner-Regiment Prinz Ludwig had a lighter blue coat with yellow facings and lining, as well as a white aiguillette on the right shoulder. Buttons were tin and arranged 1-2-1 on each lapel, plus two on each cuff. Vests were yellow and breeches buff with knee-length black gaiters. The cocked hat had a white plume, though for officers it was white-over-yellow. Musicians wore yellow coats with light-blue facings and lining, plus lace (Haarmann 1970: 140–43).

Accouterments for musketeers and grenadiers consisted of two leather belts, one (featuring a match case for grenadiers) for a cartridge pouch, the other for a short sword. Unlike the British, many German troops continued to wear one belt around the waist rather than over the right shoulder. A haversack and canteen completed the field equipment, supplemented at times by a knapsack and blanket roll. The *Jäger* company was also equipped with cartridge belly boxes.

For arms, musketeers and grenadiers were equipped with a musket, bayonet, and short sword, while the *Jäger* company carried German-manufactured rifles with sword-bayonets. It appears that most Braunschweig muskets were from the Prussian Potsdam-Spandau manufactory, or were based on the Prussian pattern from the 1730s. Dragoons also carried a broadsword, the *Pallasch*. Infantry officers and sergeants carried polearms, the blades for officers engraved with the Braunschweig cipher and horse crest, though it is unclear whether they continued to use these in North America or adopted fusils.

Colors

Braunschweig seems to have followed the Prussian system of each infantry battalion having a single colonel's color – the *Leibfahne* – plus one regimental color – the *Ordinärfahne* – per company. The basic design featured a running white horse on a red field in the center, surrounded by a golden wreath and surmounted by a crown. Each of the flag's sides featured a flame design with a burning grenade in its center, with the grenade's fuse pointing toward the center. In the corners between the flame designs were the golden ducal ciphers, wreaths, and crowns. The colors of the flag and its flames varied depending on the regiment and whether it was a colonel's or regimental color. The colonel's color was always white but with yellow flames for Prinz Friedrich, yellow for Riedesel, red for Specht, and blue or possibly green for von Rhetz. The regimental flags of Prinz Friedrich were black with yellow flames, for Riedesel yellow with blue flames, for Specht red with white flames, and for von Rhetz blue or possibly green with white flames. Dragoner-Regiment Prinz Ludwig also appear to have taken four guidons to North America; these were light blue, swallow-tailed, and featured the white horse on a red field, surrounded by a wreath and surmounted by a crown, with the cipher and laurels in four corners. Famously, the flags of the Braunschweig regiments were successfully smuggled out of Patriot captivity following defeat at Saratoga in the mattress of Riedesel's wife, Charlotte von Massow.

HESSEN-HANAU

Hessen-Hanau came into being after the conversion of the future ruler of Hessen-Cassel, Frederick II, to Roman Catholicism. Frederick's Protestant father, William VIII, wished to punish his son by reducing the lands Frederick would inherit. He therefore gave the county of Hanau-Münzenberg to Frederick's oldest son, William, who was still a Protestant. This secundogeniture created the quasi-independent state of Hessen-Hanau, ruled now by Count William, who in turn remained Frederick II's heir and thus the hereditary prince of Hessen-Cassel. Frederick II tried repeatedly to reunite Hessen in the face of his son's defiance, but to no avail. The two regions did not become one state again until 1821.

British support for William was part of what maintained Hessen-Hanau's independence, and at the instructions of George II Hanoverian soldiers occasionally helped garrison the region in defiance of pressure from Hessen-Cassel. Count William's mother – the wife of Frederick II of Hessen-Cassel – was Princess Mary, the second-youngest daughter of Britain's George II. In August 1775, not long after news of the battle of Bunker Hill (June 17, 1775) had reached Europe, Count William was the first German hereditary prince to promise to provide military assistance to Britain. Writing to George III, he initially offered a regiment free of charge, and declared rather grandly that 'all sons of the land which the protection of your Majesty alone insures to me, and all are ready to sacrifice with me their life and their blood for your service' (quoted in Lowell 1884: 15).

Talks commenced between Colonel William Faucitt and the Hessian Baron Friedrich von der Malsburg. A treaty was signed on February 5, 1776, whereby Hessen-Hanau would provide an infantry regiment of 668 men to serve the British crown, though despite William's initial claim, it would come at a price. This contingent was enlarged by a further deal signed on April 25, 1776, that added an artillery company of six guns, and again on February 10, 1777, when a corps of *Jäger* was added. Lastly, a convention on January 15, 1781, added a unit described as the Free Corps of Light Infantry, consisting of 830 men. This, along with semiregular shipments of reinforcements to replace casualties in the preexisting units, saw the contribution of Hessen-Hanau toward British manpower over the course of the war reach 2,422 men. The final sum paid to Hessen-Hanau by Britain amounted to £343,110.

Organization and deployment

The Hessen-Hanau infantry regiment, Erbprinz (not to be confused with the Hessen-Cassel Regiment Erbprinz, though William was colonel-in-chief of both), had first been raised in 1763. The contingent sent to North America consisted on paper of one battalion organized into five musketeer companies each of 109 men, a grenadier company of 111 men, and a regimental staff of 19 men. The musketeer companies each consisted of one captain, one first lieutenant, one second lieutenant, one ensign, one sergeant-major, two sergeants, one quartermaster-sergeant, one ordnance-sergeant, one color-bearer, three corporals, three drummers, and 93 privates. The grenadier company was the same but with no ensign, no color-bearer, two drummers, two second lieutenants, two fifers, and 95 privates. The regimental staff consisted of one colonel, one lieutenant-colonel, one major, one judge, one regimental quartermaster, one chaplain, one surgeon-major, three surgeons, one drum-major, six hautboys, one provost, and one provost's servant. The regiment's colonel was Wilhelm Rudolf von Gall.

The artillery company was commanded by Captain Georg Pausch, and consisted of six officers and 128 men. The British were required to supply the actual artillery pieces on campaign – these ultimately consisted of four 6-pounders, two light 6-pounders, and two light 3-pounders. The four light guns acted as battalion guns while the four 6-pounders formed a battery under Pausch. They were all bronze guns, rather than iron.

The *Jäger* corps first raised in 1777 (frequently referred to as a *chasseur* corps) was commanded by Lieutenant-Colonel Carl Adolf Christoph von Creutzbourg. It initially consisted of four companies, with a fifth added in 1778. Each company consisted on paper of one captain, one first lieutenant, one second lieutenant, one sergeant-major, one sergeant, one quartermaster-sergeant, one captain-of-arms, six corporals, one surgeon's mate, three buglers, 78 privates, and three officers' servants – apart from the colonel's company, which had one lieutenant and his servant more, and only 76 privates. The regimental staff consisted of a regimental surgeon, judge, quartermaster, adjutant, two armorers, one armorer's assistant, five wagoners, and a provost.

The Free Corps of Light Infantry raised in 1781 consisted of five light-infantry companies, one of which was armed with rifles. Each company consisted of three officers and 157 men, while the regimental staff was made up of one lieutenant-colonel, one major, one surgeon, one paymaster and his assistant, one provost, and one gunsmith. They were commanded by Lieutenant-Colonel Michael von Janecke.

The Infanterie-Regiment Erbprinz set out in March 1776 and arrived in Portsmouth on March 30. There they joined a fleet bound for Québec that included the Braunschweig corps. They arrived in Québec on June 8 and were soon joined by Captain Pausch's artillery company. The *Jäger* corps set out on March 7, 1777 (the same day the Ansbach-Bayreuth corps began their own journey into British service). The Atlantic crossing proved difficult and they reached Québec in a scattered fashion, with only one company arriving in time to participate in the campaigns of 1777.

Service history

The Hessen-Hanau corps provided notable service to the British over the course of the American Revolutionary War. Infanterie-Regiment Erbprinz and the artillery joined the Braunschweig troops as part of Burgoyne's mid-1777 offensive from Canada down the Hudson River. Captain Pausch's artillery company was employed aboard British boats during the battle of Valcour Island (October 11, 1776). Erbprinz's colonel, Gall, was promoted to brigadier-general and given command, besides Infanterie-Regiment Erbprinz, of the Braunschweig Infanterie-Regiment Prinz Friedrich, with the two combining to form the 2nd Brigade under the Braunschweig officer Major-General Friedrich Adolph Riedesel during the battles of Freeman's Farm and Bemis Heights. With Burgoyne's defeat, Erbprinz and the artillery joined the so-called Convention Army of prisoners. Much of Erbprinz was exchanged for Continental Army prisoners in 1781, and the regiment was re-formed at Québec, which it helped garrison until the end of the war.

The spontoon of a Hessen-Hanau officer carried during the 1777 Saratoga campaign. On the blade it bears the cipher "WL" for Wilhelm Landgraf. Some German states, such as Braunschweig, are thought to have abandoned the use of polearms in America, but others, like Hessen-Hanau, seem to have continued to use them in combat. (Military and Historical Images Bank)

Both Hessen-Cassel and Hessen-Hanau fielded an Infanterie-Regiment Erbprinz, and the colonel-in-chief of both, William, was the heir of Hessen-Cassel and the ruler of Hessen-Hanau respectively. The Hessen-Cassel regiment was until 1780 a fusilier unit wearing miters, while the Hessen-Hanau regiment wore distinctive looped lace. (Staatsarchiv Braunschweig H VI 6 Nr. 27)

The difficulties of the transatlantic crossing meant the Hessen-Hanau *Jäger* did not participate with the main body of Burgoyne's expedition, but the first company to arrive was able to join a supporting operation in upstate New York. Under First Lieutenant Jacob Hildebrand they played an important role at the bloody battle of Oriskany (August 6, 1777), and participated in the siege of Fort Stanwix (August 2–22, 1777). Afterward they spent the rest of the war patrolling the Canadian frontier, with little in the way of active fighting.

The Free Corps of Light Infantry arrived at New York in 1781. It remained as part of the New York garrison until the end of the war, then returned home and was disbanded in July 1783.

Uniforms and personal equipment

Soldiers of Infanterie-Regiment Erbprinz wore a dark-blue coat in the Prussian style, with red facings and lining (some sources claim the facings were pink, but this seems to have been a mistake). Buttons were white. The six buttons on each coat lapel were arranged in three pairs, surrounded by white lace in the "Brandenburg" style, looped in figure eights, with tasseled ends. A seventh button with the same style of lace was worn below each lapel, with another pair above each cuff, and a pair on each pocket.

Vests and breeches were straw-colored, with black full-length gaiters. Neck stocks for all ranks were black. Musketeers wore cocked hats with scalloped white lace, a red-and-yellow pompom, and a black cockade. Grenadiers wore tall white metal-fronted caps with yellow backing cloth and white piping, crowned by a red tuft topped by a yellow circle with a red middle. Officers' lace was silver, while their waist sashes were silver with horizontal crimson stripes. Gorgets were silver and bore the red-and-white-striped lion rampant of Hessen, armed with a sword, on a blue background, along with the "WL" cipher of William Landgraf. Both officers and sergeants wore white gauntlet-gloves.

Privates, corporals, and sergeants were equipped with whitened leather belts to secure a black leather cartridge pouch on the right hip and a short sword, plus attendant scabbards, on the left. The sword-belt was most likely worn around the waist rather than over the right shoulder. Linen haversacks, calfskin knapsacks, and canteens were also issued.

The sergeants were ostensibly each equipped with a halberd and disciplinary cane, though it is unclear if these were taken into action. Officers were equipped with spontoons bearing the "WL" cipher, though again it is unknown if they swapped these for fusils in action Infanterie-Regiment Erbprinz was partially equipped with muskets from a procurement from the Pistor manufactory at Schmalkalden by Hessen-Cassel, supplemented with firearms procured from small-scale manufacturers.

Soldiers of the Hessen-Hanau artillery company wore dark-blue Prussian-style coats with red facings and lining, white vests, and gaitered trousers, possibly with red-and-white vertical stripes. They had black cocked hats with white lace, black cockade, red pompom, and tasseled cords. Officers had gold hat cords and wore silver sashes with red horizontal stripes.

The Hessen-Hanau *Jäger* wore dark-green coats with red facings and lining, plus dark-green vests and straw-colored breeches with full-length, dark-brown gaiters. They had unlaced black cocked hats with black cockades. Officers had silver sashes with red horizontal stripes. Cartridge pouches and belly boxes were black leather, while belts were brown leather. The Hessen-Hanau *Jäger* rifles were produced by the Pistor manufactory.

The Free Corps of Light Infantry was uniformed in dark-green coats without lapels, with red cuffs and collars. The rifle-armed company had leather caps for headwear, while the rest had cocked hats (Haarmann & Holst 1963: 40–42).

Colors

Infanterie-Regiment Erbprinz likely followed the Prussian tradition of one color per company in each battalion, with the company commanded by the colonel having a distinct flag. For Erbprinz, all of these were rose-pink and without the "flame" designs featured on many other German states' flags. The center was dominated by the red-and-white striped lion rampant of Hessen-Hanau, which faced toward the flag staff, the opposite direction to the red-and-white striped lion rampant of Hessen-Cassel.

The Hanau lion lacked the crown borne by the Cassel lion, but wielded a white sword in its left paw. It was surrounded by silver laurel wreaths with red berries, and surmounted by a crown and motto, *HASSORUM GLORIA*. On the colonel's color, the lion was set against a large ducal shield crest within a heraldic "mantle and pavilion," surmounted by a crown and flanked by two golden, crowned lions rampant. In the four corners of both the colonel's and company flags was the cipher of Count William, flanked by silver laurels and surmounted by a crown.

(continued on page 33)

A

HANNOVER

1: Lieutenant-General August de la Motte
2: Gibraltar medal
3: Officer, Regiment von Reden
4: Private, Regiment de la Motte

B

BRAUNSCHWEIG

1: Color-bearer, Infanterie-Regiment Prinz Friedrich
2: Private, Leichtes Infanterie-Bataillon von Barner
3: Private, Dragoner-Regiment Prinz Ludwig

C

HESSEN-HANAU
1: Grenadier, Infanterie-Regiment Erbprinz
2: Cannoneer, Hessen-Hanau Artillery Company
3: Light infantryman, Hessen-Hanau Freikorps

D

WALDECK

1: Drummer, 3rd English-Waldeck Regiment
2: Musketeer, 3rd English-Waldeck Regiment
3: Grenadier, 3rd English-Waldeck Regiment

E

ANSBACH-BAYREUTH
1: Grenadier, Ansbach Regiment
2: NCO, Ansbach-Bayreuth Artillery Detachment
3: Officer, Bayreuth Regiment

1

2

3

F

ANHALT-ZERBST
1: Grenadier, 1778
2: Musketeer, 1778
3: Musketeer, 1781

RIFLE-ARMED TROOPS
1: Braunschweig *Jäger* sergeant
2: Hessen-Hanau *Freikorps* rifleman
3: Private, Ansbach-Bayreuth Feldjäger Korps

WALDECK

Waldeck was a small German state of approximately 37,000 inhabitants lying west of Hessen-Cassel. Its ruler, Prince Friedrich Karl August, wrote to George III in November 1775, offering his assistance in quashing the American Revolution. Karl August himself had campaigned in Austria and was a lieutenant-general in the Dutch service. Waldeck had a tradition of supplying auxiliary regiments to the Dutch military, and the rebellion in America provided an opportunity for its prince to make further military investments. A treaty was concluded between Britain and Waldeck at Arolsen on April 20, 1776.

Organization and deployment

Waldeck supplied one regiment of one battalion, accompanied by two battalion guns, for service in North America. The state already had two regiments serving the Dutch military, so to form what was termed the 3rd English-Waldeck Regiment, officers and men were transferred over from the two preexisting units, with the ranks then further supplemented by a recruiting drive.

The regiment's official strength consisted of one battalion of one grenadier and four musketeer companies. Each musketeer company consisted of one captain, one first lieutenant, one ensign, three officers' servants, one surgeon's mate, three sergeants, one quartermaster-sergeant, one master-at-arms, one color-bearer, six corporals, three drummers, 107 privates, and one supernumerary. The grenadier company was composed of one captain, one first lieutenant, one second lieutenant, three officers' servants, one surgeon's mate, three sergeants, one quartermaster-sergeant, one master-at-arms, six corporals, three

A buckle plate used to secure the waist belt of a Waldeck soldier. It bears the cipher "FF" for *Fürst Friedrich*, the ruler of Waldeck. (The New York Historical Society/ Getty Images)

drummers, two fifers, 110 grenadiers, and one supernumerary. The regimental staff consisted of one lieutenant-colonel, one major, two captain-lieutenants, one adjutant, one auditor, one quartermaster, one chaplain, one surgeon, one drum-major, four musicians, one provost and his servant, and two drivers. The 3rd English-Waldeck Regiment therefore consisted of a total of 670 men, plus two bombardiers and 12 cannoneers for the two 3-pounder battalion guns. The official establishment also permitted 32 women. The regiment's colonel was Johann Ludwig Wilhelm von Hanxleden. Prince Karl August gifted each man in the regiment a hymn book before their departure.

After a two-week delay, the Waldeck Regiment marched approximately 130 miles north to Bremerlehe, lying on the Weser River, where they were to embark on transports. The Waldeckers arrived on May 30, 1776, and next day were met by Colonel William Faucitt, who inspected the troops and administered their new oath of allegiance to King George III. Faucitt wrote a report for his superior detailing his impressions of the Waldeck Regiment:

> The Front and Rear Ranks of this Regt. are compos'd of stout, tall, well-made fellows, but the Outer ranks are in general very short, consisting chiefly of lads furnish'd by the country of Waldeck, some of whom appear'd rather too young and too slight for immediate service; there also seem'd several old men in the Corps. The whole however seem'd full of spirits and good will. The Grenadier Company is a very fine body throughout, and made a very shewy [sic] appearance with their caps fac'd with black Bear skin: the appointments in general are rich and handsome, and the clothing (blue, with light yellow facings & cuffs & white waistcoats and breeches) arms and accoutrements not only complete but quite new & very good. As far as these articles will go, it must be confess'd the Prince has spared no expence [sic] to put his regiment upon the best footing. (TNA SP 81/184)

There were insufficient British vessels to carry the Waldeck Regiment, so three Dutch vessels, *Jacob Cornelius*, *Benjamin*, and *John Abraham*, were hired. They transported the regiment to Britain, departing on June 3. They arrived off Portsmouth on June 20, where they were provided with a fourth transport, *Adamant*, to ease the overcrowded conditions on the other ships. Originally, British planners had intended to deploy the Waldeck Regiment to Canada, but changed the unit's destination to New York to tie in with plans to retake that city from revolutionary forces. The Waldeck expedition therefore joined a larger fleet that departed Portsmouth on June 28. They reached Sandy Hook, New Jersey, on October 18, continued on to New York the day after, and disembarked on October 22. From there the Waldeckers took small boats to join the main Crown Forces army under Lieutenant-General Sir William Howe near New Rochelle.

Service history
The 3rd English-Waldeck Regiment served as part of the main Crown Forces army in North America during the remainder of the New York campaign of 1776. The unit's first contact with revolutionary forces

occurred close to the village of Maroneck, New York, on October 27, where Waldeck pickets consisting of a corporal and 18 privates were attacked. The corporal and two privates were captured, while two more were seriously wounded and left behind.

The Waldeck Regiment was brigaded with troops from Hessen-Cassel. The Waldeckers' first major engagement was the storming of Fort Washington on November 16, 1776, where the regiment suffered six men killed and 16 wounded. During the winter of 1776/77 the Waldeckers occupied quarters in Elizabeth, New Jersey, and were involved in the sharp skirmishing that plagued the area. In June they were shifted to Staten Island, where they helped defeat a rebel attack on August 23, 1777. They saw little further action until they were redeployed on November 3, 1778, first to Jamaica, where they spent a month, and then on to Pensacola in West Florida, arriving on January 17, 1779. The intention was for the Waldeck Regiment to help garrison the frontier between British and Spanish colonial possessions on the Mississippi River, but insufficient transports meant the Waldeckers had to be ferried there in company detachments, one after the other.

On June 21, 1779, while they were still in the process of doing so, Spain declared war on Britain. Unaware of this, on September 4 the company under Captain Alberti was taken prisoner by the Spanish aboard their transports while traversing Lake Pontchartrain. Alberti and several other officers, three sergeants, one drummer, and 49 privates were seized and taken to New Orleans, then on to Spanish holdings in Mexico and then Cuba. Alberti died soon after his capture from a fever. Those of his men who survived the climate largely remained in captivity until they were exchanged in 1782.

The fortunes of the rest of the Waldeck Regiment continued in a similar vein. A small force left to delay a Spanish offensive at the crumbling Fort Bute was swiftly captured on September 7, 1779, along with more of the regiment when the British commander of the post at Baton Rouge surrendered on September 21. In a skirmish near Mobile Bay on January 7, 1781, Colonel von Hanxleden, his adjutant, and two rank and file were killed, and one captain, one sergeant, and five rank and file were wounded.

The siege of Pensacola (March 9–May 10, 1781) marked the end of military operations for the Waldeck Regiment. The Crown Forces garrison capitulated, and what remained of the regiment was captured, a total of 11 officers, nine staff, 14 sergeants, 13 corporals, 11 musicians, 219 privates, and nine artillerymen. Throughout both their time as garrison troops or in Spanish captivity, the Waldeck Regiment suffered grievous losses to disease and malnutrition – ten times as many men to the inimical climate as it did to direct Spanish military action. Reinforcements were shipped from Waldeck each year that the war progressed, but they were insufficient to maintain the regiment at full strength.

Many of those Waldeckers captured at Pensacola were permitted to return to New York, on the condition that they would no longer fight against Spain. They remained there for the rest of the war, performing garrison duties. While on Long Island they received new colors after the previous ones were surrendered to the Spanish. These were presented to the regiment while in winter quarters at Flatbush, Long Island, on January 21, 1783, though the exact design of the flags remains unknown.

An example of a hanger, or short sword, carried by Waldeck soldiers. Though dating from 1794, the design was unchanged from the Revolutionary period. (Penta Springs Limited/Alamy Stock Photo)

Artwork of a Waldeck soldier in 1794. The uniform remained very similar to the one worn by the 3rd English-Waldeck Regiment during the American Revolutionary War. (Hansrad Collection/Alamy Stock Photo)

With the war in North America at an end by summer 1783, on July 16 the Waldeck Regiment, by this time consisting of 15 officers, seven staff, 20 sergeants, 31 drummers, 335 rank and file, 20 women, and 13 children, embarked on transports that would return them to Europe. They left New York on July 25 and reached Britain one month later. They carried on to Bremerlehe on September 3, and from there marched back to Waldeck. The last Waldeck troops involved in the war, the new recruits for the year 1782 that had spent time garrisoning Halifax, Nova Scotia, reached home on October 10, 1783.

Uniforms and personal equipment

Like all other German auxiliaries involved in the American Revolutionary War besides those from Anhalt-Zerbst, the Waldeck Regiment broadly followed the Prussian style. Regimental coats were dark blue with yellow facings and lining. Six white-metal buttons were arranged 1-2-3 on each lapel plus a further three below each lapel. The coat also had two buttons on each cuff and two on each sleeve immediately above the cuff. Vests and breeches were white, as were the knee-high gaiters worn with the breeches. Cocked hats were trimmed with white wool edging and completed by yellow cords. Grenadiers wore black bearskin caps, without metal-plate fronts. Sergeants were distinguished by silver lace and cords on their cocked hats, silver epaulets, and silver sword-knots. Musicians wore yellow coats with blue facings, trimmed with lace, silver in the case of the drum-major. Reportedly, the uniforms of the surgeon's mates were the same as those of enlisted men, but their coats had no facings. Drivers wore blue suits with yellow lining. Artillerymen wore blue coats with yellow buttons, red facings, and buff vests and breeches, with bombardiers distinguished by gold epaulets.

Accouterments for musketeers consisted of two leather belts, one for a cartridge pouch, the other for a bayonet and short-sword scabbards, plus haversacks and canteens, supplemented at times by furred knapsacks and blanket rolls. As early as February 19, 1776, the Pistor manufactory was contracted to supply 300 muskets, plus sabers and belts for Waldeck. Two shipments were made to Arolsen by the end of April, and further replacement arms were supplied by Pistor in 1778 and 1782 (Moller 2011a: 424–25). Some muskets may also have been supplied during the state's previous Dutch service.

ANSBACH-BAYREUTH

During the period of the American Revolutionary War, Ansbach-Bayreuth was actually two margraviates, Brandenburg-Ansbach and Brandenburg-Bayreuth, located in the Franconian region and ruled jointly by Margrave Christian Friedrich Karl Alexander von Ansbach. Alexander's holdings were heavily in debt, so the margrave was receptive to British financial offers in exchange for the use of Ansbach-Bayreuth's small standing army in North America. Colonel Faucitt arrived at the Ansbach court on January 14, 1777, and a treaty was duly signed with Britain on February 1, whereby Ansbach-Bayreuth supplied a force of two single-battalion infantry regiments (one from Ansbach and one from Bayreuth), one *Jäger* company, and one artillery company of two field guns and their attendant crews in exchange for a sum eventually totaling more than £100,000.

Organization and deployment

The Ansbach regiment, sometimes referred to as the 1st Regiment, was commanded by Colonel Friedrich Ludwig Albrecht von Eyb, and the Bayreuth regiment, or 2nd Regiment, by Colonel August Valentin von Voit von Salzburg. They were therefore called the Regiment von Eyb and the Regiment von Voit, at least initially. Colonel von Eyb returned to Uffenheim in Ansbach in May 1778, and command of the 1st Regiment was taken over by Colonel von Voit, while Voit's position as commander of the 2nd Regiment was taken up by Colonel Johann Heinrich Christian Franz von Seybothen. The Regiment von Eyb therefore became the Regiment von Voit and the original Regiment von Voit became the Regiment von Seybothen from May 1778 onward (Döhla 1990: xviii).

Both Ansbach-Bayreuth infantry regiments consisted of one grenadier and four musketeer companies, totaling 570 men. The musketeer companies consisted of 112 men each, the grenadier company of 113, and the regiment staff of nine individuals – the colonel, major, chaplain, auditor, surgeon-major, regimental quartermaster, drum-major, provost, and assistant provost. The regular musketeer companies each consisted of one captain, one first lieutenant, and two second lieutenants as well as two sergeants, one quartermaster-sergeant, five corporals, one surgeon, one fifer, two drummers, one tent attendant, and 95 privates (Döhla 1990: xviii).

The initial *Jäger* company deployed to America in 1777 was commanded by Captain Christoph von Cramon. It totaled 101 men and consisted of one captain, one first lieutenant, two second lieutenants, two sergeants, one quartermaster-sergeant, five corporals, one medic, one tent attendant, and 87 *Jägers*. Four other *Jäger* companies were raised in Ansbach-Bayreuth over the course of the war – the second in 1779, the third in 1781, and the fourth and fifth in 1782 – creating a *Jäger* regiment that was placed under the command of Lieutenant-Colonel Christoph Ludwig von Reitzenstein. Among the ranks of the later companies was Lieutenant August Neidhardt von Gneisenau, who went on to become a prominent Prussian field marshal.

The Ansbach-Bayreuth artillery company was commanded by First Lieutenant (later Captain) Hoffmann and consisted of one lieutenant, four bombardiers, eight conductors, one tent attendant, and 30 cannoneers, split between two field guns (Döhla 1990: xix).

The Crown Forces Monument at Guilford Courthouse mentions the Ansbach-Bayreuth *Jägerkorps*. (US National Park Service)

Hessen-Kassel Regiment von Bose
det. Hessen-Kassel Jägerkorps
det. Ansbach-Bayreuth Jägerkorps
det. 17th Regiment of Light Dragoons
British Legion Cavalry
Royal North Carolina Regiment

After an address from Margrave Alexander, the Ansbach-Bayreuth troops set out from their homeland on March 7, 1777, marching north to their embarkation point on the Main River at Ochsenfurt. Conditions were poor, with insufficient room on the riverboats transporting the troops, and a mutiny ensued among the two infantry regiments. Margrave Alexander himself traveled north to quell the unrest. The *Jägers* under Captain von Cramon began to restore order, and there was a brief firefight, resulting in one soldier killed and two wounded from the Regiment von Voit. Falling into line first, Regiment von Eyb, particularly the grenadier company, then helped restore discipline to the Regiment von Voit.

The Ansbach-Bayreuth troops traveled by sea to Dordrecht in the Netherlands, where they took the oath that saw them formally enter into British service. They boarded British ships and sailed first for Portsmouth, then on to North America.

Service history

The Ansbach-Bayreuth corps arrived off New York on June 3, 1777, and made landfall at Staten Island two days later. The British commander-in-chief in North America, Lieutenant-General Sir William Howe, was quoted by his Hessian aide-de-camp, Captain Friedrich von Münchhausen, as saying that "the Anspachers [*sic*] are exceedingly tall and handsome fellows. Without doubt these Anspach [*sic*] regiments are the tallest and best-looking regiments of all those here" (quoted in Döhla 1990: xvii).

Their first major operation involved being assigned to a force sent north up the Hudson River in October, with the intention of providing support for the Burgoyne Expedition that had been launched from Canada in June. Burgoyne had already surrendered, however, and the contingent returned to New York having seen little action.

The Ansbach-Bayreuth regiments were then deployed to British-occupied Philadelphia in November 1777, but again were not heavily engaged. When the British evacuated the city on June 18, 1778, the Ansbach-Bayreuth troops returned to New York by ship rather than overland with the rest of the Crown force, thereby missing the battle of Monmouth (June 28, 1778). They arrived at Long Island on June 20.

On July 15, 1778, the corps landed at Newport, Rhode Island, to assist its small garrison. On August 29 they clashed with the combined Franco-American forces attempting to retake the area, and remained in Newport for the rest of 1778 and much of 1779.

Rhode Island was evacuated in October 1779, and the Ansbach-Bayreuth corps returned to New York, spending the next year-and-a-half performing garrison duties occasionally punctuated by raids into the interior. In May 1781 the regiments were selected to be part of the reinforcement sent to Virginia to assist General Charles Cornwallis's efforts in the south, under the initial command of Colonel von Voit. They were involved in the siege of Yorktown (September 28–October 19, 1781), acting as a rearguard during Cornwallis's failed breakout attempt on October 16. They surrendered with the rest of the garrison, and most of them were not released until May 1783.

As the war progressed, disease and desertion took a heavy toll on the numbers of the Ansbach-Bayreuth corps, and they had to be replenished by regular shipments of new recruits. Margrave Alexander provided yearly reinforcements to bolster the preexisting regiments, along with particular surges following new agreements and further payments from the British in 1779 and 1782. While the initial contribution consisted of 1,285 men, it is estimated that a total of 2,353 Ansbach-Bayreuth soldiers served in North America between 1777 and 1783. Of that number almost half, 1,170, died, deserted, or were given leave to remain in America at the conclusion of hostilities (Döhla 1990: xx).

Uniforms and personal equipment

The uniforms of the Ansbach-Bayreuth corps followed the Prussian style that had become popular in many parts of Europe following the Seven Years' War. Both infantry regiments wore a dark-blue coat with red lining and "white" (pewter) metal buttons as well as a white vest, white breeches, and full black linen gaiters; musketeers wore a laced cocked hat while grenadiers wore a white metal-fronted cap. The Regiment von Eyb (later von Voit) had red facings, while the Regiment von Voit (later von Seybothen) had black facings. Accouterments consisted of two whitened leather belts, one for a cartridge pouch, the other for a bayonet and short sword plus scabbards, plus haversacks and canteens, supplemented at times by knapsacks and blanket rolls.

An Ansbach-Bayreuth flag, one of a number captured following the surrender at Yorktown. (Military and Historical Images Bank)

The *Jäger* wore a green coat with red facings, red lining, and yellow-metal buttons with a green vest, buff breeches, and full black linen gaiters; their cocked hats were unlaced while their leather accouterments, including cartridge pouches, were brown. Artillery personnel wore a blue coat with red facings, red lining, white-metal buttons, white vest, white breeches, and full black linen gaiters, plus a laced cocked hat.

Exactly where the majority of the Ansbach-Bayreuth weaponry was sourced from remains unclear, but it is known that pistols were purchased from the manufactory at Potsdam-Spandau, while the rifles of the Ansbach-Bayreuth *Jäger* seem to have come from the Pistor manufactory at Schmalkalden (Moller 2011a: 424).

Colors

The Ansbach-Bayreuth flags appear to have been white, and lacked the flame-like design common to many German military standards of the period. A color captured at Yorktown shows a laurel and a palm forming a wreath tied with a pink ribbon, framing the cipher "MZB" for *Markgraf zu Brandenburg*. Above it is a crown, and beneath it is the date 1775, presumably when the flag was issued. On the reverse is an eagle carrying a marshal's baton and palm and laurel branches beneath a scroll featuring the motto *PRO PRINCIPE PATRIA* – "for prince and fatherland."

ANHALT-ZERBST

Anhalt-Zerbst was a small German state with a population of about 20,000, lying between Saxony and Prussia. Its ruler was Prince Friedrich August, the younger brother of the Russian Empress Catherine the Great. Prior to her marriage to the Russian Czar Peter III, Catherine had been named Sophie Friederike Auguste von Anhalt-Zerbst-Dornburg – she was the daughter of Christian August, the ruler of Anhalt-Zerbst prior to Friedrich inheriting the title in 1747. Friedrich served in the military of the Holy Roman Empire, becoming a general of cavalry and a *Reichs-General-Feldmarshall-Lieutenant*. For most of his life he lived in Basel in Switzerland or in Luxembourg, ruling his princedom via written directives and decrees issued to the privy councilors responsible for its day-to-day running. He was the last German ruler to sign a military treaty with Great Britain, in October 1777. Anhalt-Zerbst would supply two infantry battalions in the Regiment Princess von Anhalt, sometimes known as the Regiment von Rauschenplatt after its commander, a total of 1,160 men.

Organization and deployment

Unlike all of the other German states that provided Britain with military assistance during the American Revolutionary War, Anhalt-Zerbst followed the Austria military model of organization and tactics, rather than that of Prussia. Like the Austrian Army, the first battalion raised by Anhalt-Zerbst for service in North America included two grenadier companies rather than one, though it is unclear whether there were also four musketeer companies, or three. Four was the standard in an Austrian Army battalion, but a total of six companies would result in a number beyond the 625 men who reported for embarkation at Stade. Given the high number of deserters beforehand, however, it seems feasible that the battalion's composition was indeed four musketeer and two grenadier companies.

If using the Austrian system, a regular musketeer company from the Regiment Princess von Anhalt would have included one captain, one lieutenant, one second lieutenant, one *Feldwebel* (senior NCO), one quartermaster, five corporals, two quartermaster orderlies, four musicians (three drummers and one fifer), ten *Gefreite* (first-class privates), one pioneer, and 109 musketeers. Grenadier companies were organized similarly but had four corporals, two drummers, no first-class privates, two fifers, and 84 grenadiers instead of 109 musketeers.

Interestingly, accounts in 1778 mention a *Jäger* corps commanded by a Captain Nuppenau operating in Canada, and supposedly originating from Anhalt-Zerbst. No detailed information exists about this unit, or about the supposed existence of Anhalt-Zerbst artillery; if there was any artillery sent to North America, it was likely two light (3-pounder) "battalion guns" used to support the regiment, a standard Austrian practice.

The Regiment Princess von Anhalt was inspected for the first time in November 1777 by Colonel William Faucitt, the British Army officer responsible for conducting the majority of negotiations with the various German rulers contracting troops to George III. He wrote that the regiment:

was compos'd of a fine body of men all young, robust and well put together, but they handled their arms, march'd & wheeled not so well as I cou'd have wish'd. I made them go through the firing motions likewise, which they also perform'd but indifferently. The Commanding Officer, however, Colonel Rauschenplat, assured me that the greatest part of them had not been call'd in from their furloughs for above three or four days, having been absent from the Regiment for the greatest part of the year, and that by diligent drilling for the time they might have before their march, he wou'd be responsible for their being brought to a proper degree of perfection for any service. I am inclin'd to think this might be very well accomplish'd within the course of ten days or a fortnight, especially as the Colonel appear'd to be a very active intelligent Officer, who had serv'd all the last War in the Austrian Army. Their Clothing was white with red facings and cuffs, and in general very good; their arms the same, and clean. The Grenadiers wore bear-skin caps; there are two companies of them to each Regiment. Upon the whole they made a handsome appearance, and did not seem to want for good will, especially the Officers, at least as many as I saw of them, several being absent. (Quoted in Sartorius 1999: 31)

Recruiting poster from the first half of the 18th century showing an Anhalt-Zerbst grenadier and infantryman. (Unknown/ Wikimedia/Public Domain)

Faucitt's observation about the men being young was accurate, as it seems the vast majority, around 900, were new recruits, rather than transfers from other regiments or veterans reenlisting.

Prussia refused to allow German troops bound for British service to march through its territory on their way to costal embarkation points, and due to Anhalt-Zerbst's geography, the Regiment Princess von Anhalt was forced to take a somewhat circuitous route to reach Stade, where it was set to board ships. This led to a great deal of misadventure – in the village of Zeulenrode an attempt to apprehend a deserter led to an innkeeper's wife being accidentally killed, resulting in a riot. Predatory Prussian recruiting parties also descended on the regiment, enticing away new soldiers. By the time the regiment approached Stade, 334 men had deserted, though conversely about 130 new men were enlisted on the long march, leaving a force of 625 men, plus 31 women on the official muster. This force embarked at Stade on April 22, 1778, sailing two days later. They arrived at Portsmouth on May 12 and joined a convoy bound for Québec, departing on May 25. Following a stop at Torbay until June 13, they arrived at Québec on September 5 (Lowell 1884: 52).

Popular myth holds that the British commander in Canada, Lieutenant-General Sir Guy Carleton, had not been told to expect troops from Anhalt-Zerbst. Worried about landing soldiers he was not authorized to employ, he forced the contingent to remain on their ships for three months while seeking clarification from Britain. This story appears to be pure fabrication – in reality the Regiment Princess von Anhalt disembarked on September 8, three days after arriving.

Service history

The Anhalt-Zerbst regiment never saw serious action during the American Revolutionary War, spending its time on garrison duties in Canada and New York. In a letter to George Germain, 1st Viscount Sackville, Secretary of State for the Colonies, dated September 13, 1779, Major-General Sir Frederick Haldimand, a senior British officer, wrote that

> the German troops are ill calculated for American service and, being uninterested in the event of the war, are little to be depended on. The regiment of Anhalt-Zerbst, the best of them, is but a regiment of recruits; very few of these troops can be employed anywhere in this country except on garrison duty, and even in that way they are helpless in many respects. (TNA CO 42/39/261)

That same month, Prince Friedrich August offered to raise another regiment for British service. A small number of reinforcements had already been dispatched earlier that year, and more would go in 1780 and 1782, but August's proposed regiment was considerably larger. The British rejected his proposal, but agreed to an enlarged reinforcement of the Regiment Princess von Anhalt. This force would total one major, one first lieutenant, six second lieutenants, three surgeons, 15 NCOs, 25 *chasseurs* (light infantry), 383 privates, one servant, 21 woman, and 12 children. On April 20, 1781, it was embarked at Bremerlehe on three transports. The contingent departed on May 11 for New York, arriving three months later to the day.

Seven privates perished during the voyage, and many more became ill – 112 men were admitted to hospitals when the regiment arrived in New York – while the rest disembarked at Brooklyn Ferry on August 14, 1781. They were quartered at Wallabout and Bushwick on Long Island for four days, then were ferried to Paulus Hook, New Jersey, to take the place of the British 54th Regiment of Foot. While garrisoning the area, the unit's commander, Major Rudolph Heinrich von Lüttichau, had his men swap their footwear and cloth breeches with shoes and linen trousers due to the heat and the difficulty of weekly marches into New Jersey to forage.

Interestingly, the Hessen-Hanau artillery officer Captain Georg Pausch claimed that though the Anhalt-Zerbst regiment's drill was that of the Austrian military, when drilling with German units from other states they adopted the Prussian drill to match their auxiliary allies.

The regimental augmentation left New York on July 25, 1783, arriving in Britain on August 25. From there they took transports for Stade, arriving on September 8 and disembarking on September 10. The main body of the regiment in Québec embarked on seven transports on August 2, 1783, sailing first to the Isle of Bic on the St. Lawrence River, and then on to Portsmouth, which they reached on September 10. They sailed from the Downs on September 12 and reached Bremerlehe one week later, then carried on to the town of Jever in Lower Saxony where they were to perform garrison duties. The 1782 batch of recruits, the last to be sent from Anhalt-Zerbst, arrived in Halifax, Nova Scotia, from Bremerlehe on August 13, 1782, and stayed there as a garrison force consisting of one lieutenant, one sergeant, 41 privates, and one woman. They left on August 2, 1783, sailing to Stade. By October 1783, the last of the 984 remaining men of the regiment had all returned home.

Uniforms and personal equipment

As noted, Anhalt-Zerbst followed the military organizations and style of Austria rather than Prussia, and this was reflected in their uniforms and equipment. The standard uniform was a white regimental coat with red lapels, cuffs, and lining (it did not have a collar), plus a red strap on the left shoulder. Buttons were brass (often described as "yellow") and arranged with seven on each lapel, two beneath each lapel, two on each cuff, three on each pocket and one on each side of the back. Vests were red and breeches white, with knee-length black gaiters. It seems some modifications were made in North America – a description in 1778 states the Anhalt-Zerbst troops wore buff trousers and short white gaiters. Black cocked hats were surmounted by a white plume. Grenadiers wore black bearskin caps with a front plate inscribed with the cipher "FA" for Friedrich August. The back of the cap was red cloth with yellow piping.

The British Army's Major Frederick Mackenzie made an intriguing observation as to the uniforms of the Anhalt-Zerbst corps in New York, writing:

Friedrich August, ruler of Anhalt-Zerbst and brother to Empress Catherine II of Russia, is depicted in this 1785 engraving by J.C.G. Fritsch (1720–1802). A soldier in the service of the Holy Roman Empire, he spent little time in Anhalt-Zerbst, preferring to rule from his other holdings. (INTERFOTO/Alamy Stock Photo)

> The Anhalt Zerbst troops looked more like Dragoons than Infantry. They are clothed in white, faced with Red, Felt Caps, a la Hussar; Boots, and a Red Cloak. Their Arms are a Musquet, & bayonet, and a short Sword. Over their Waist belts, which are buckled over their coats, they wear a kind of Sash of red & yellow worsted. They are good looking, well sized young men. (Mackenzie 1968: 589)

It has been speculated that this rather grandiose uniform was worn by "pandurs," irregular troops originating in Hungary that served the Habsburg Empire. Anhalt-Zerbst's ties to Austria make this possible – it may be that while personnel of the first battalion serving in Canada were uniformed along more standard regulations, those of the second battalion helping to garrison New York were indeed pandur irregulars.

The Pistor manufactory at Schmalkalden supplied 500 muskets, 100 rifles, and 500 sidearms to Anhalt-Zerbst in 1778. Pistols were also purchased from Potsdam, raising the possibility that more muskets were bought there as well (Moller 2011a: 425).

Colors

Records exist of an 18th-century Anhalt-Zerbst infantry color destroyed during World War II. It was white, with a red flame design running inward from each of the four edges, though these flames were shorter and thicker than many German colors of the period due to the size of the central device. The flag's middle was taken up by the Anhalt-Zerbst crest, which was divided into two halves – on the left were the colors of Saxony; on the right, the right half of a red eagle on a silver field. The crest was framed with a laurel held together by a ribbon at the bottom.

SELECT BIBLIOGRAPHY

Decurion (1937). "The Hanoverian Regiments in India, 1782 to 1792," in *The Journal of the United Service Institution of India*, Vol. 67: 205–15.

Döhla, Johann Conrad, ed. Bruce E. Burgoyne (1990). *A Hessian Diary of the American Revolution*. Norman, OK: University of Oklahoma Press.

Dornfest, Walter (1983). "Hanoverian Troops in the British Service, 1775–1792," in *Journal of the Society for Army Historical Research*, Vol. 61, No. 245: 58–61.

Eelkin, Max von, ed. (1868). *Memoirs, and Letters and Journals, of Major General Riedesel, During his Residence in America*. Albany, NY: Joel Munsell.

Eelkin, Max von (1893). *The German Allied Troops in the North American War of Independence, 1776–1783*. Albany, NY: Joel Munsell's Sons.

Haarmann, Albert W. (1970). "Notes on the Braunschweig Troops in British Service During the American War of Independence, 1776–1783," in *Journal of the Society for Army Historical Research*, Vol. 48, No. 195: 140–43.

Haarmann, Albert W. & Donald W. Holst (1963). "The Hessen-Hanau Free Corps of Light Infantry," in *Military Collector and Historian*, Vol. XV: 40–42.

Lowell, Edward J. (1884). *The Hessians and the Other German Auxiliaries of Great Britain in the Revolutionary War*. New York, NY: Harper & Bros.

Mackenzie, Frederick (1968). *Diary of Frederick Mackenzie, Volume II*. New York, NY: Arno Press.

Moller, George D. (2011a). *American Military Shoulder Arms Volume I: Colonial and Revolutionary War Arms*. Albuquerque, NM: University of New Mexico Press.

Moller, George D. (2011b). *American Military Shoulder Arms Volume II: From the 1790s to the End of the Flintlock Period*. Albuquerque, NM: University of New Mexico Press.

Sartorius, C.A., trans. H.J. Retzer (1999). "Journal of the Hessen-Hanau Erbprinz Infantry Regiment Kept by 2nd Lieutenant Carl August Sartorius, Regimental Quartermaster, translated by Henry J. Retzer," in *Journal of the Johannes Schwalm Historical Association*, Vol. 6, No. 3: 26–34.

The National Archives, UK: Colonial Office, Class 42, Vol. 39.
The National Archives, UK: State Papers, Class 81, Vol. 184.

PLATE COMMENTARIES

A: SENIOR COMMANDERS
(1) Major-General Friedrich Adolf Riedesel, Freiherr zu Eisenbach
Major-General Friedrich Adolf Riedesel (sometimes misspelled in secondary sources as von Riedesel) was one of the most senior officers from the German states serving the British Crown during the American Revolutionary War. The commander of the Braunschweig corps sent to North America, he was a Seven Years' War veteran and the *Freiherr* (baron) of the town of Eisenbach. He held overall command of all German state troops during the 1777 Saratoga campaign during which, despite notable service, he and most of his troops were captured. Exchanged midway through the Revolutionary War, he resumed command of forces around New York, but did not see active campaigning again. Riedesel is here depicted in his major-general's uniform, which largely mirrors the uniforms of the rest of the Braunschweig corps in its lack of lace and ornamentation. The white feathers adorning his silver-laced, cocked hat denote that he is a general officer.

(2) Colonel Johann Friedrich Specht
Colonel Johann Friedrich Specht commanded one of the four Braunschweig musketeer regiments deployed to Canada in 1776. During the Saratoga campaign, Specht commanded the 1st Brigade of the German corps, consisting of three Braunschweig infantry regiments – his own (commanded in the field by Major Carl von Ehrenkrook), von Rhetz, and Riedesel. Specht wears the uniform of his regiment, identified by the red facings. His silver sash worked with yellow is indicative of the types of sash worn by Braunschweig officers. His gorget, like that worn by Major-General Riedesel, bears the running white horse on a red field crest of Braunschweig – almost identical to that of Hannover.

(3) Colonel Wilhelm Rudolf von Gall
Colonel Wilhelm Rudolf von Gall was born in Hessen-Cassel in 1734 and served as a junior officer in the Hessian Army during the Seven Years' War. Following the war's conclusion he became colonel of Infanterie-Regiment Erbprinz, the only musketeer regiment deployed by Hessen-Hanau to North America during the American Revolutionary War. Gall wears the uniform of an officer of his regiment, most readily identifiable by the distinctive silver "Brandenburg"-style figure eight lace, as well as the scalloped lace on the cocked hat. Like other Hessen-Hanau officers, his sash is silver worked with red stripes, and his silver gorget bears the red-and-white striped lion rampant, similar yet distinct from the crest of Hessen-Cassel.

B: HANNOVER
(1) Lieutenant-General August de la Motte
Born in Braunschweig-Wolfenbüttel on November 17, 1713, August de la Motte joined the Hanoverian Army and fought in the Seven Years' War. Ranking as a colonel in October 1775, he was chosen to lead a Hanoverian infantry brigade and sent to Gibraltar. During the grueling siege (June 24, 1779– February 7, 1783), de la Motte served as third-in-command of the garrison, being promoted to lieutenant-general in 1781. He returned to Hannover in October 1784 and died in Verden on August 29, 1788. Here we see the diminutive de la Motte during the latter part of his time at Gibraltar, his lieutenant-general's uniform closely following the British style.

(2) Gibraltar medal
The Defence of Gibraltar Medal was privately instituted by General Sir George Augustus Eliott, the garrison commander, to commemorate the role played by Hanoverian troops in the successful defense of Gibraltar.

(3) Officer, Regiment von Reden

His uniform betraying strong British influences, this officer of the Regiment von Reden wears the black facings of his unit and the gorget, epaulet, and officer's waist sash denoting his rank. The Hanoverian troops deployed to the Mediterranean acquitted themselves well, on the whole, and crucially replaced British regiments urgently needed in North America.

(4) Private, Regiment de la Motte

This private of the Regiment de la Motte wears the pale-yellow facings of his unit. His hat decoration, long white gaiters, and waist belt with "hanger" distinguish his appearance from that of the British infantrymen he otherwise resembles. His coat is a "brick red" color several shades duller than the scarlet worn by the two officers.

C: BRAUNSCHWEIG
(1) Color-bearer, Infanterie-Regiment Prinz Friedrich

This subaltern – or junior officer – carries one of the four *Ordinärfahnen* belonging to the Braunschweig Regiment Prinz Friedrich. In its center is the Braunschweig crest of the running white horse, while the cipher of the ducal ruler occupies each corner. Many Braunschweig flags famously avoided capture after Saratoga due to being smuggled out in the mattress of Major-General Riedesel's wife. The Regiment Prinz Friedrich largely avoided the campaign, though – it seems to have been considered the most subpar of the Braunschweig regiments, and was assigned garrison duty at the recently recaptured Fort Ticonderoga.

(2) Private, Leichtes Infanterie-Bataillon von Barner

Besides the *Freikorps* from Hessen-Hanau and the possible existence of Anhalt-Zerbst pandurs – neither of which saw significant action in North America – Braunschweig-Wolfenbüttel was the only German state to provide Crown Forces with a dedicated light-infantry battalion rather than a *Jäger* corps consisting of multiple *Jäger* companies. Consisting of five companies in total, Light Infantry Battalion Barner's second company was a *Jäger* company, but the other four were musketeer companies. These troops do not appear to have functioned as light infantry in the truest sense, but were armed with smoothbore muskets and bayonets, and were expected to provide close support to the *Jägers*, who were vulnerable to close assaults. The light-infantry musketeers were uniformed and equipped in keeping with the other Braunschweig musket-armed troops, distinguished by black collars, black cuffs, and a black shoulder strap on the left shoulder.

(3) Private, Dragoner-Regiment Prinz Ludwig

The only cavalry regiment deployed by any German state during the American Revolutionary War, Dragoner-Regiment Prinz Ludwig sailed to North America without horses, expecting to receive them on arrival. In reality, acquiring mounts proved difficult, and many of the cavalrymen were killed or captured at the battle of Bennington while fighting on foot, on an operation intended to seize more horses. Not all of the regiment was destroyed, however, and a small number equipped with mounts continued to act as couriers, videttes, and provide close protection for senior officers during the Saratoga campaign. While dispensing with their riding boots when operating on foot, Prinz Ludwig dragoons maintained their cavalry swords, of a type known as a *Pallasch*, as well as a musket and bayonet.

D: HESSEN-HANAU
(1) Grenadier, Infanterie-Regiment Erbprinz

The Hessen-Hanau Regiment Erbprinz is often confused with the Hessen-Cassel Regiment Erbprinz – the former were musketeers, and the latter fusiliers, so their headwear was the most obvious difference, with the Hanau musketeers wearing cocked hats and the Cassel fusiliers metal-fronted caps. The situation is rendered more complex, however, in the case of the Hessen-Hanau grenadiers – like most German grenadiers, they wore metal-fronted caps very similar to fusiliers, albeit grenadier caps tended to be slightly taller, and fusilier caps tended to be topped by a small spike whereas grenadiers' caps were surmounted by a pompom. More distinctive, as far as the Hanau regiment was concerned, were the "Brandenburg"-style figure eight lace loops on the regimental coats. It should also be noted that while some secondary sources claim the regiment's facings were pink, they appear to have in fact been red.

(2) Cannoneer, Hessen-Hanau Artillery Company

The Hessen-Hanau corps provided the most artillery of any German state bar Hessen-Cassel, though the pieces themselves were provided by the British. Of the eight cannon, the four lighter guns were used as battalion guns, employed in close support of the infantry, while the other four – bronze 6-pounders – were combined to form a battery. The

While this image depicts a British soldier in Canada during 1776, similar clothing was likely worn by those German troops left garrisoning Canada during the winter months. (Staatsarchiv Braunschweig H VI 6 Nr. 27)

Hessen-Hanau artillery served with distinction during the Saratoga campaign under the command of Captain Georg Pausch, including service onboard boats during the battle of Valcour Island (October 11, 1776). This cannoneer was tasked with performing any of the many roles required not only in servicing the artillery in combat, but in maintaining and moving it when out of action. He is distinguished by his coat's red facings and brass buttons, as well as the brown leather belly box for his musket's ammunition.

(3) Light infantryman, Hessen-Hanau Freikorps

The *Freikorps* were units employed by various German states from the mid-18th century onward. While their exact nature and composition varied greatly in the early years, they tended to consist of either deserters, adventurers, or ethnic minorities such as Hungarians and Croats or Balkan Muslims who were either forbidden from joining regular regiments, or did not wish to. Ideally, *Freikorps* swapped discipline and regimentation for greater tactical and strategic flexibility, and could be employed as light infantry or partisans. Lack of discipline was a double-edged sword, however, and *Freikorps* tended to be viewed as unreliable and substandard troops, and could be relegated to garrison duties. Hessen-Hanau provided a *Freikorps* regiment for Britain late in the war. The exact regimental composition and the nature of its troops remains unknown, but it seems they were uniformed in green coats with red facings and lining. The Hessen-Hanau Freikorps spent its short time in North America helping to garrison New York.

E: WALDECK
(1) Drummer, 3rd English-Waldeck Regiment

The drummers of the 3rd English-Waldeck Regiment wore reversed colors, yellow regimental coats with blue facings, trimmed with extra lace. Note also the unusual positioning of the four buttons on the coat cuff and sleeve, a feature unique to Waldeck among the German troops that served in the American Revolutionary War. The brass-plated drum bears the "FF" cipher of Waldeck. As well as relaying orders on the battlefield, drummers were often the ones assigned to mete out corporal punishment, a recourse usually taken by German troops with slightly (though not excessively) higher frequency than in British regiments.

(2) Musketeer, 3rd English-Waldeck Regiment

This Waldeck musketeer's coat, like those worn by the rest of the regiment, has yellow facings and lining. He carries typical campaign kit, including a cloth haversack, canteen, and animal-hide knapsack, slung over his right shoulder. Waldeck troops saw extensive service in the southernmost British colonies of North America. There, the inimical climate claimed far more lives than the invading Spanish. Those Waldeck troops who survived usually spent long periods in Spanish prisons before being exchanged near or at the end of the war.

(3) Grenadier, 3rd English-Waldeck Regiment

A report by the British Colonel William Faucitt after he inspected the 3rd English-Waldeck Regiment before they departed from their homeland indicated that the grenadier company wore bearskin caps rather than completely metal-fronted ones, including a brass plate with the Waldeck crest. Alongside Anhalt-Zerbst they were therefore the only German grenadiers to wear bearskins. The grenadier cartridge pouch, as well as having a central, brass oval plate bearing the Waldeck insignia, also had a flaming grenade crest in each

corner of the flap. Faucitt described the grenadiers as being particularly fine and making a showy appearance, and that the regiment overall was well uniformed and equipped, albeit some of the men were a little slight or young, and a few too old.

F: ANSBACH-BAYREUTH
(1) Grenadier, Ansbach Regiment

The joint German state of Ansbach-Bayreuth provided one musketeer regiment consisting of two battalions for British service during the American Revolutionary War, one from the province of Ansbach, and one from the province of Bayreuth. Both included a grenadier company, ostensibly consisting of the largest and bravest men in each battalion. The practice of actually equipping them with grenades, except in unusual circumstances such as sieges, had died out many decades previously. Like most other German grenadiers of the period, this grenadier from the Ansbach regiment wears a tall cap, plated with silver inscribed with the black eagle and crown of his ruler, Margrave Karl Alexander. British officers were initially impressed by the Ansbach-Bayreuth corps, describing them as the best-looking of any of the German troops with the main British force operating in North America.

(2) NCO, Ansbach-Bayreuth Artillery Detachment

The Ansbach-Bayreuth musketeer regiment appears to have been accompanied by a small artillery detachment, which most likely served as battalion guns, light pieces that were intended to supplement the firepower of the infantry and provide mutual support to each other. This artillery NCO is equipped with a straight-bladed sword, secured with a white knot with black stripes. He also carries a partisan polearm. The Ansbach-Bayreuth artillery surrendered with its infantry regiment at Yorktown.

(3) Officer, Bayreuth Regiment

The uniform of this officer of the Bayreuth battalion of the Ansbach-Bayreuth Regiment includes a number of badges of rank – a silver aiguillette on his right shoulder, and silver lace, as well as a silver waist sash and sword knot, worked with black, distinctive to officers from Ansbach-Bayreuth. Note that he lacks a gorget. Not all officers wore gorgets on campaign, possibly finding them impractical or too clear a mark for enemy sharpshooters. Like many militaries of the period, there is little in this uniform to distinguish battalion-level officers such as ensigns, lieutenants, and captains from one another – enlisted men were expected to show deference to all. The officer is armed with both a sword and a spontoon, its blade bearing the crest of the Margrave of Ansbach-Bayreuth. Unlike the British, the NCOs and officers of some German states appear to have continued to use polearms while on campaign in North America.

G: ANHALT-ZERBST
(1) Grenadier, 1778

This Anhalt-Zerbst grenadier showcases the similarities between Anhalt-Zerbst uniforms and the uniforms of nearby Austria. Rather than the dark blue favored by all of the German states involved in the American Revolutionary War bar Hannover, the infantry coats worn by Anhalt-Zerbst were white and, in the case of the Regiment Princess von Anhalt, bore red facings. Instead of grenadier caps with brass or silver front plates, Anhalt-Zerbst grenadiers wore bearskins.

These uniform choices reflected the fact that Anhalt-Zerbst's ruler had closer diplomatic relations with Austria and the Holy Roman Empire than he did with Prussia, the military model for most other minor German states. Like other Anhalt-Zerbst infantry regiments, the Regiment Princess von Anhalt had two grenadier companies. Almost all depictions of German grenadiers of the period show them as mustachioed – some commentators regarded a good moustache as a sign of experience and reliability.

(2) Musketeer, 1778

The uniforms of musketeers belonging to the Anhalt-Zerbst regiment sent to North America were similar to those of the grenadiers, with white coats faced with red and red vests, albeit the cocked hat was worn instead of the bearskin. Seemingly the musketeers also wore white gaiters with white overalls or trousers. The buttons for the regiment were brass, and the coats had Swedish-style slit cuffs. Stocks were black, but with white edging.

(3) Musketeer, 1781

This is the style of Anhalt-Zerbst musketeer as documented by one British officer late in the war. The unusual uniform is described as being more akin to that of a dragoon than an infantryman, and may represent the garments of a pandur, a type of irregular light infantry employed by the Habsburg Empire and some of its allies. Of note are the felt hussar cap, the red-and-yellow worsted sash, the black "cuffed" boots, and the red cloak, a luxurious item rarely issued to regular infantrymen. Unfortunately, no other clear accounts exist of this particular uniform, and nor did these troops ever see service beyond garrisoning New York in the latter years of the war. It is difficult to say how commonplace this attire was without further documentation.

H: RIFLE-ARMED TROOPS

(1) Braunschweig *Jäger* sergeant

Along with Hessen-Cassel, Hessen-Hanau and Ansbach-Bayreuth, Braunschweig-Wolfenbüttel provided *Jäger* light infantrymen to Crown Forces serving in North America. These elite, rifle-armed skirmishers and marksmen provided valuable service to the British, particularly in the more forested and difficult areas of North American terrain, and earned a reputation as some of the best troops on either side. While a green uniform was a prerequisite for all *Jäger* regardless of their state of origin, there were subtle differences between the different *Jäger* corps. The coats of Braunschweig *Jäger* were unique insomuch as the buttons on their lapels were spaced in a 1-2-1 pattern, and also bore Swedish-style open-sided cuffs – designs which mirrored the uniforms of regular Braunschweig troops. As a sergeant, this *Jäger* also carries a cane – a symbol of authority and corporal punishment – and wears gloves. Despite being a sergeant, he is still equipped with a rifle, and expected to be at least as proficient with it as his subordinates, if not more so.

(2) Hessen-Hanau *Freikorps* rifleman

The Hessen-Hanau *Freikorps* seems to have included a company of rifle-armed soldiers, emphasizing their likely role as light infantry. With belly boxes for ammunition, green coats with red facings and lining matching those of the rest of the regiment, they would have appeared similar to the *Jäger* of other states at a glance. Rather than a cocked hat, however, they wore leather caps bearing the cipher of Erbprinz Wilhelm of Hessen-Hanau. The wearing of such caps was more

This image depicting a Canadian farmer reveals more details of the cold-weather dress likely worn by the German auxiliary troops stationed in Canada. Overcoats such as this were sometimes made from cut-up blankets, and provided greater protection against winter weather than standard regimental coats. (Staatsarchiv Braunschweig H VI 6 Nr. 27)

in-keeping with the practices of British light infantry, who wore leather caps similar to the style of jockey caps from the period. Despite being rifle-armed and possibly capable in irregular warfare, it would appear these troops saw little to no active combat.

(3) Private, Ansbach-Bayreuth Feldjäger Korps

Ansbach-Bayreuth supplied a large number of *Jäger* throughout the course of the war – initially just one company with the first expedition in 1777, but then four more over the next five years. Combined these formed a regiment, or *Feldjäger Korps*, the largest contingent of such light infantrymen besides those sent by Hesse-Cassel. Among them was the Saxony-born Lieutenant August Neidhardt von Gneisenau, who would eventually become one of Prussia's most prominent field marshals during the Napoleonic Wars (1803–15). This Ansbach-Bayreuth *Jäger* is uniformed like all other *Jäger* with a dark-green coat with crimson facings and lining and a dark-green vest. His coat buttons are brass and grouped in pairs. His black cocked hat includes a green cockade, while his leatherwork is brown. Like all other *Jäger* he is armed with a rifle, in this case likely produced at the Pistor manufactory at Schmalkalden. Such weapons proved vital in allowing Crown Forces to combat the riflemen employed by American revolutionary commanders.

INDEX

References to illustration captions are shown in **bold**. Plates are shown with page and caption locators in brackets.

AXIS OCCUPATION FORCES (1)
1: *Küstenjäger*, Küstenjäger-Abteilung `Brandenburg', Rhodes, July 1943
2: *Gefreiter*, Jäger-Regiment 724, Agrinio, June 1943
3: *SS-Sturmmann*, SS-Polizei-Panzergrenadier-Regiment 7, Larissa, June 1944

AXIS OCCUPATION FORCES (2)
1: *Caporale*, 13° Reggimento di fanteria `Pinerolo', Kastoria, November 1942
2: *SS-Unterscharführer*, SS-Pionier-Bataillon 4, Kozani, July 1944
3: *Carabiniere*, VI Battaglione Carabinieri Reali, Messolonghi, March 1943

F

BULGARIAN OCCUPATION FORCES
1: *Podpolkovnik*, 7th Infantry Division, Thessaloniki, March 1943
2: *Rednik*, 16th Infantry Division, Xanthi, October 1942
3: *Polkovnik*, 11th Infantry Division, Komotini (Gjumjurdschina), June 1941

G

COLLABORATIONIST FORCES
1: *Evzon*, 2nd Security Regiment, Patras, May 1944
2: *Ypostràtigos*, 1st Security Regiment, Athens, September 1943
3: Militiaman, *Lòchos Asfaleias*, EES, Kozani, March 1944

ITALIAN OCCUPATION FORCES

Following Greece's capitulation to the Axis forces, Italy, whose army had suffered 63,000 casualties in six months of bloody fighting against the Greek Army in the Pindus Mountains and Albania, was assigned the largest part of mainland Greece (as well as the Ionian Sea islands, the south Aegean Sea islands and the easternmost corner of Crete). Contrary to the widespread perception (itself the product of post-war historical revisionism) that the Italians were 'benevolent occupiers', Fascist Italy's short-lived occupation of Greece was harsh, with Italian forces responsible for atrocities not unlike those committed by their German and Bulgarian allies. The contempt with which the average Greek treated the Italian occupiers, and the concerted efforts of the first collaborationist government of Lieutenant-General Gheorghios Tsolakoglou to drive a wedge between Italy and its German allies, frustrated, to an extent, Italy's occupation agenda, thereby weakening its grip on the part of Greece under its nominal control.

Fascist Italy divided Greece into three occupation zones: the Ionian Sea islands, the south Aegean Sea islands and mainland Greece. These were ruled directly by Italy; by contrast, the Germans had appointed a collaborationist government to represent, politically, the interests of occupied Greece, and to handle its administrative matters. The Ionian Sea islands came under Italy's direct political, economic and military control, with the medium- to long-term aims of their 'Italianization' and annexation (Italy had applied the same tactic with the Dodecanese islands, which it had annexed following the Italo-Turkish War of 1911–12). A similar policy of forced Italianization was also followed for the south Aegean Sea islands, where a cultural, administrative and economic separation process was instituted, in preparation for their integration into the Dodecanese. These unpopular measures and ineffective annexation efforts were to cost the inhabitants of the south Aegean Sea islands dearly, as supplies ran low and economic activity ground to a halt. Italy's policy vis-à-vis the Greek Jews living under its control was more

BELOW LEFT
Two smartly dressed Italian infantry officers (from left to right, an elderly *colonello* and a youthful *tenente*) pose for the camera, in a photograph taken at an unidentified location in Greece, in March 1942. They are both turned out in standard, officers' quality Italian infantry service uniforms (their tailor-made tunics are cut from fine gabardine, so-called *cordellino* material), and carry holstered Beretta M34 service pistols, the Italian armed forces' standard sidearm, issued to officers, NCOs and machine-gun crews. (Author's Collection)

BELOW RIGHT
Taken in Athens, at the Herodes Atticus Odeon, in June 1942, this photograph shows Italian and German troops attending what appears to be an official event (the Italian officers sitting in the front rows of the Roman amphitheatre carry their ceremonial swords). (Author's Collection)

This Italian soldier wears the M40 uniform while on guard duty, most likely in Athens, in December 1942. He is equipped with a 6.5mm Mannlicher-Carcano M1891 rifle, a bayonet, twin ammunition pouches and an M33/34 helmet. (Author's Collection)

A haggard-looking, off-duty Italian infantry soldier, in a superior quality, pre-war, M33-pattern service uniform (note the black collar), in Omonoia Square in Athens. The photograph is dated 9 June 1943. (Author's Collection)

ambivalent, resulting in some innocent lives being spared. It is unclear, however, whether this policy was an indication of benevolence vis-à-vis the Greek Jews or an attempt to demonstrate Italy's autonomy of action with respect to the Germans.

Italian occupation forces in mainland Greece had the dubious distinction of being those upon whom the incipient Greek resistance movement cut its teeth. Italian supply convoys were routinely attacked, and their more isolated troop concentrations ambushed. Also, it was Italian troops that garrisoned the Gorgopotamos River railway bridge, with some 30 of them being killed during the successful sabotage operation, reinforcing German prejudices against their Italian allies. Prejudices aside, the Italians never managed to tackle the guerrilla problem in those parts of Greece under their responsibility: the Igoumenitsa–Metsovo–Trikala Road, the only major west–east communication artery in Italian-occupied mainland Greece, was under constant guerrilla attacks and never safe to use, even for armoured columns.

The Italian occupation forces' reaction to the guerrilla problem swung between the irresolute and the disproportionate: following guerrilla attacks, Italian troops would be dispatched to the mountains only to return, in many cases, empty-handed. This induced punitive actions, mostly at the initiative of local commanders, which neither deterred fresh guerrilla raids nor secured the cooperation of the locals. In December 1942, Italian forces burned the villages of Chrysso and Mikro Chorio and executed most of their residents. In February 1943, it was the turn of Domeniko to be razed to the ground, with 194 civilians, including women and children, murdered. In March 1943, Italian forces razed the village of Tsaritsani and executed 40 of its inhabitants; and in June 1943, in retaliation for the blasting of a rail tunnel in the vicinity of Kournovo, the Italians arrested and executed 106 civilians. Already in the summer of 1943, the Italians had withdrawn their garrisons from Greece's countryside, concentrating their forces within the larger urban centres. Unsurprisingly, this facilitated guerrilla activities.

By the time of Italy's surrender, and the demise of the 11ª Armata, between 70 and 80 per cent of the Italian Occupation Zone in Greece was under effective guerrilla control. Thanks to the surrender of the 24ª Divisione di fanteria 'Pinerolo' and the Reggimento 'Lancieri di Aosta' (6°) but also earlier incidents – such as the battle of Bougazi on 4-6 March 1943, during which ELAS forces captured and disarmed an entire Italian battalion – the *andartes* were able to replenish their supply of arms and ammunition from Italian stocks. Italy's surrender had catastrophic consequences for the men of, among others, the 33ª Divisione di fanteria 'Acqui' in Cephalonia, several thousands of whom perished at the hands of their former allies, after their commander, Generale di divisione Antonio Gandin, refused to surrender to the Germans. A similar fate befell the officers of the Italian garrison of the island of Kos.

In summary, the performance in Greece of the Italian armed forces (whose organization, uniforms and equipment have been explored in detail in earlier Osprey publications) was unspectacular, both as an occupation and as an anti-partisan force, the morale of its members low and the quality of their command sub-standard (as reflected in the near-total breakdown of the Italian officers' authority over their troops after Italy's surrender).

11ª Armata (Generale d'armata Carlo Vecchiarelli; total establishment: 7,000 officers and 165,000 rank and file, of which around 90,000 in mainland Greece, as follows):
III Corpo d'armata (HQ: Thebes): 36ª Divisione di fanteria da montagna 'Forlì' (HQ: Athens); 24ª Divisione di fanteria 'Pinerolo' (HQ: Larissa); Reggimento 'Lancieri di Aosta' (6°); Reggimento 'Lancieri di Milano' (7°); Comando truppe Italiane Euboea (HQ: Halkis).
VIII Corpo d'armata (HQ: Agrinio): 33ª Divisione di fanteria 'Acqui' (HQ: Argostoli, Cephalonia); 56ª Divisione di fanteria 'Casale' (HQ: Aetolikon); 29ª Divisione di fanteria 'Piemonte' (HQ: Patras); 59ª Divisione di fanteria da montagna 'Cagliari' (HQ: Tripoli)
XXVI Corpo d'armata (HQ: Ioannina): 37ª Divisione di fanteria da montagna 'Modena' (HQ: Arta); 18° Reggimento di fanteria 'Acqui' (HQ: Corfu); 2° Gruppo alpini 'Valle' (HQ: Ioannina)
Comando Egeo (Rhodes): 6ª Divisione di fanteria 'Cuneo' (HQ: Samos); 50ª Divisione di fanteria 'Regina' (HQ: Rhodes and Kastellorizo)
Comando truppe Italiane Creta (Italian forces under the command of Heeresgruppe E, in Crete): 51ª Divisione di fanteria 'Siena' (HQ: Neapolis, Lasithi); Brigata speciale 'Lecce' (HQ: Kato Horio)
Comando Militare Marittimo della Grecia occidentale (HQ: Patras)
Comando Aeronautica della Grecia (HQ: Athens)
* Not including Carabinieri, Milizia Volontare per la Sicurezza Nationale, Guardia di Finanza units and support services.

BULGARIAN OCCUPATION FORCES

On 1 March 1941 the Kingdom of Bulgaria signed the Axis Tripartite Pact. Soon thereafter, German forces entered Bulgaria via Romania, in preparation for Hitler's invasion of Yugoslavia and Greece. On 20 April 1941, following the collapse of the Greek defences, Bulgarian troops (10th Infantry Division, 2nd Border Guards Brigade and 1st Army Reserve Regiment) crossed into Greece and, without a formal declaration of war, occupied the Greek prefectures of Serres, Drama, Kavala and Rhodope as well as parts of the Evros prefecture (eastern Macedonia and western Thrace minus those parts of the Evros prefecture that bordered Turkey, which were occupied by the Germans). On 14 May 1941, Bulgaria annexed those territories, with the forbearance of the Germans but without their definitive support, creating the *oblast* (region) of Belomorska Thrakia ('White Sea' or Aegean Thrace), a new Bulgarian province of ten districts with a total population of 640,000 inhabitants, stretching from the Strymon (Struma) River in the west, to a straight line connecting the Greek coastal city of Alexandroupolis (Dedeağaç) to the Bulgarian town of Svilengrad in the east. Sofia thus realized one of its unfulfilled territorial aspirations – access to the Aegean Sea – and increased its territory by about 13,000 square kilometres (the equivalent of over one third of the total area of Belgium).

In July 1943, the Germans allowed Bulgaria to expand its zone of control to also include central and parts of western Macedonia (the territory westwards of the hitherto Bulgarian Occupation Zone, stretching from the Axios (Vardar) River, in the west, to the Strymon River, in the east), as well as Halkidiki (minus the Mount Athos Peninsula). These areas were neither annexed to, nor administered by, Bulgaria, which was to operate there under German supervision (in truth, the Bulgarians overstepped their mandate and only reluctantly withdrew from areas they had invested with their troops, incurring the displeasure of their German patrons). Thessaloniki and an area of 32km around it remained under German control, with the headquarters of the Bulgarian 7th Infantry Division stationed just outside the city limits.

A Bulgarian naval infantryman stands guard above Limenas, on the northern coast of the island of Thassos, facing the Thracian coast. Between 1941 and 1944, Bulgaria garrisoned Thassos and the smaller island of Samothraki with three naval-infantry regiments – two in Thassos and one in Samothraki – as well as coastal-artillery and infantry units. Bulgarian Navy uniforms had a distinct Imperial Russian look about them and had evolved the least from their historical antecedents compared to those worn by men serving with Bulgarian Army and Air Force units. (Bulgarian Archives State Agency/Wikimedia/Public Domain)

ABOVE LEFT
A Bulgarian military band, at the time of the German invasion of Greece. All of its smartly dressed members (including the goggle-wearing junior officer leading it) wear the M36 *kaska*, the standard-issue Bulgarian Army helmet until the outbreak of World War II, but also widely in use during the conflict, only partly replaced by the slightly modified M41 variant. (Author's Collection)

ABOVE RIGHT
Bulgarian and German soldiers at a mixed-troop gathering. Judging by their orderly appearance, the Bulgarians visible here must belong to a front-line (as opposed to a mobilized) unit, among those positioned along the border with neutral Turkey for the duration of World War II. Of interest are the *bustina*-type forage caps worn by the Bulgarian soldiers, complete with a stylized lion badge on the front and a shield in Bulgaria's national colours on the right-hand side. (Author's Collection)

Bulgaria's official policy throughout its Occupation Zone was one of forced 'Bulgarianization', for those amenable to it, and of expulsion or extermination, for those who opposed it. It is telling that, by late 1941, over 100,000 Greeks had left or been forced out of the Bulgarian Occupation Zone; by the end of the war, this number had nearly doubled. Those unwilling to abide by this policy and adopt Bulgarian nationality were deported, after being forced to 'cede' their ancestral homes to the Bulgarian state.

The policies pursued by the occupation authorities caused great resentment, both in Athens (the seat of the Greek puppet government) and within the occupied territories themselves, where an uprising broke out on 28 September 1941, first in the city of Drama and then throughout eastern Macedonia. Following violent clashes between ELAS forces and the Bulgarian police and gendarmerie, Bulgarian troops of the 14th and 39th Infantry regiments seized all men aged between 18 and 45, executed over 3,000 of them in Drama alone (another 10,000 to 12,000 were executed across the countryside, over a period of several weeks) and destroyed entire settlements. The 'Drama Massacre' and the brutal reprisals across eastern Macedonia expedited the exodus of the civilian population from the Bulgarian Occupation Zone into the German Occupation Zone. In March 1943, the Bulgarian occupiers also deported most of the Greek Jews living in their Occupation Zone: it is telling that, of the 780 Jewish deportees from the city of Drama, only 39 survived the Nazi death camps (Bulgaria and Romania did not protect foreign Jews living under their respective control).

The forces (mainly reserve infantry units) that Sofia committed to the occupation of Macedonia and Thrace were considerable, testifying to its concern to secure, at all costs, the new accretions to its territory. Although their numbers fluctuated over time, from about 70,000 in June 1941 to roughly 40,000 in September 1944, they remained substantial throughout the three-year period of the Bulgarian occupation. Bulgarian infantry divisions, of which 12 existed at the start of World War II and 22 by its end, consisted of three infantry regiments each (in turn divided into three infantry battalions, each with three infantry companies, one machine-gun company with 12 medium machine guns, one mortar company with nine 81mm mortars and one anti-tank company with six 20mm guns), one artillery regiment and one anti-aircraft battery with 15 20mm guns.

To complement their occupation forces, the Bulgarians also relied, within their Occupation Zone, on Bulgarian police, gendarmerie and *Ohrana* (secret police) units as well as on paramilitary formations, including the 'Bulgarian Legion'. In early 1942, they also obtained the permission of the German High Command (Thessaloniki) to set up militias in areas outside their Occupation Zone (central and western Macedonia) by recruiting willing members of the local Slavic-speaking minority; at least three militia detachments – so-called 'Ohrana battalions' – were formed in the course of 1943 in the districts of Italian-controlled Kastoria, and German-controlled Edessa and Florina. Greek males of military age were also conscripted into the Bulgarian Army, but mostly assigned to so-called 'construction battalions' – forced-labour units – some of which operated within former Yugoslav territories also under Bulgarian occupation.

Bulgarian occupation troops – largely reservists, as the first-line units of the 3rd Bulgarian Army were stationed in positions along the border with neutral Turkey for most of World War II – conducted anti-partisan operations alongside their German allies, mostly under German command. These actions occurred during Operation *Panther* in the autumn of 1943, to clear the Metsovon Pass and Mount Olympus areas as well as the Edessa–Florina road, and Operations *Wulf, Horrido, Rentier* and *Iltis* in the spring of 1944, around the time of the launch of the SOE-mandated Operation *Noah's Ark*.

The Bulgarian Occupation Zone was home to several guerrilla bands, which occasionally clashed with the occupation forces, causing them significant attrition. The two main armed resistance organizations in the Bulgarian zone of control were ELAS and the right-wing EAO, led by

A group of Bulgarian gendarmes, policemen and soldiers, dressed in an assortment of uniforms, some of pre-World War II pedigree, pose with two of their 'trophies', most likely in the vicinity of Drama, in the immediate aftermath of the local uprising against Bulgarian rule. This photograph testifies to the barbarity with which the Bulgarian occupation authorities went about curbing the uprising, and to the absence of humanity and self-reflection displayed by those involved in restoring Bulgarian authority over occupied Macedonia. (Athens War Museum)

Greek partisans, most likely members of the right-wing EAO, led by Antonis Fosteridis, pose for the camera in their mountain sanctuary. EAO was mainly composed of Turkophone Pontic Greeks, with partisan warfare experience against the Ottoman Turks in the mountains of the Black Sea coast of Asia Minor. The men visible here appear to be dressed in traditional, black-coloured Pontic Greek costumes. Until the Tanzimat reforms of the mid-19th century, the non-Muslim subjects of the Ottoman Empire were to wear dark colours only, to distinguish them from Muslims who, as first-class subjects, were allowed a wider choice of colours. (Athens War Museum)

Antonis Fosteridis (locally known by his Turkish nickname Anton Çavuş, i.e. 'Sergeant Anton'). EAO was primarily composed of Turkophone Pontic Greeks, with partisan warfare experience against the Ottoman Turks in the mountains of Asia Minor's Black Sea coast during 1914–22. Fosteridis, a former rural constable, had his stronghold in the area between Mount Falakro and Mount Lekani (Çal-dağ) in the prefectures of Drama and Kavala, respectively, from where he conducted operations both against ELAS (as of January 1944) and the Bulgarian occupiers. EAO was established with the help and encouragement of the British, who also supplied it with arms and clothing and had BLOs assigned to it. The most important engagement that EAO fought against the Bulgarians was the battle at the Papades bridge on the Nestos River, during 7–11 May 1944: this involved an attempt by a Bulgarian battalion to interdict EAO's collection of a supply drop on Mount Kara-Dere. In charge of a group

Bulgarian occupation forces' selective orders of battle, April 1941–October 1944*

30 April 1941–October 1942: 1st Bulgarian Army (formerly 2nd Bulgarian Army; HQ: Plovdiv) garrisons annex eastern Macedonia and western Thrace with the 1st, 7th, 9th, 11th (mobilized), 13th and the locally recruited 16th Infantry divisions.

October 1942–July 1943: 1st Bulgarian Army moves to Serbia, leaving the 16th Infantry Division, reinforced by the 68th Infantry Regiment plus units of the 1st and 10th Infantry divisions, to form the (provisional) Belomorski/Aegean Corps (Major-General Trifon Y. Trifonov; HQ: Xanthe). The headquarters of the 7th Infantry Division moves to Thessaloniki, under German command, with its units (the 13th and 41st Infantry regiments, the 1st Army Reserve Regiment, the 12th Divisional Heavy Machine Gun Battalion, the 12th Artillery Regiment, the 7th Depot Regiment and the 12th Engineer Battalion) occupying the area between the Strymon (Struma) and the Axios (Vardar) rivers.

July 1943–October 1944: Under the perceived threat of an Allied invasion of Greece, the newly established Bulgarian II Corps (HQ: Drama), consisting of the 7th, 16th and 28th (mobilized) Infantry divisions, transfers to the Aegean province (where it relieves the Aegean Corps) and remains in position until its disbandment at the end of September 1944 and Bulgaria's withdrawal from Greece in early October 1944.

* Not including paramilitary forces

of 80 *andartes*, Fosteridis ambushed the Bulgarians as they were crossing the Papades bridge. Reportedly, more than 150 Bulgarian soldiers were killed in the ensuing three-day battle.

On 9 September 1944, a bloodless coup conducted by the Communist-dominated 'Fatherland Front' coalition transformed overnight the Bulgarian Army in Greece from an occupation force into an ally. Bulgarian troops evacuated Greece only reluctantly, in late October 1944, after the Soviet Union's 3rd Ukrainian Front had reached the Bulgarian border from the direction of Romania, and only days before the last of the German troops had withdrawn north to avoid becoming cut off in the Balkan Peninsula.

COLLABORATIONIST FORCES

Greece's wartime collaboration phenomenon is sensitive and analytically complex, and it cannot be explored in detail in a work of such modest length. Suffice to say that collaborators acted out of radically different motives: there were those who collaborated out of ideological (i.e. National Socialist) convictions; those who did so out of pure opportunism; and others who were driven by anti-Communism or nationalism (including irredentism). The heterogeneous motivation of Greek collaborators also reflected itself in their unit organization and activities, which ranged from the military, in the case of armed collaborationist formations sanctioned by the Greek puppet government, to the outright criminal, in the case of many of the paramilitary formations. Geographic considerations and distance from the central administration also played a significant role in the set-up, organization and activities of collaborationist formations.

Citing security concerns, the Axis occupiers initially opposed the formation of indigenous armed collaboration units. They had earlier allowed the recruitment and arming of 'Volunteer Gendarmes', grouped into several *Ethelontiki Chorofylaki* (Volunteer Gendarmerie) units, and gradually absorbed by the Gendarmerie. Five battalions (two in Athens and one each in Corinth, Kalamata and Argos) of 19 companies were created, with a total establishment of 1,600 men. These operated under the command of the German *Ordnungspolizei*, with the task of maintaining order and countering subversive elements. Units of the *Astynomia Poleon* (City Police), including the 700-strong Athens-based *Mihanokinito Tmima Astynomias Poleon* (Police Motorized Squadron), also played a prominent collaborationist role.

The first of Greece's dedicated collaborationist military formations saw the light of day in May 1943, when the Germans granted permission to the puppet government of Ioannis Rallis to establish the 1st Evzones Battalion (HQ: Athens). The importance of this unit only became apparent to its German patrons after Italy's surrender to the Allies: faced with a lack of manpower to police occupied Greece against the growing threat of its resistance movement, the Germans came to accept, out of necessity, the creation of home-grown, armed collaborationist forces. The 1st Evzones Battalion was to provide the nucleus for the raising, between September and December 1943, of a further three *Tágmata Asfalías* (security battalions). By the end of the war, a total of nine security battalions had been established, grouped in two regiments, with their headquarters in

A member of the Republican (formerly Royal) Guard, at the iconic Unknown Soldier Monument (Athens Royal Palace) during the occupation. The ceremonial Republican Guard was to serve as the nucleus for the raising, in the latter part of 1943, of the collaborationist 'security battalions', the official armed extension of the Greek puppet government. (Author's Collection)

Athens and Patras, respectively. While formally answerable to the Greek puppet government, the security battalions were armed and trained by the Germans, operating under the overall command of Generalleutnant der Waffen-SS Walter Schimana, the *Höherer SS- und Polizeiführer* for Greece. Their men (pejoratively called *'Germanotsoliades'* or 'German Evzoni') donned the uniforms of the Evzoni (see Plate H1) and swore an oath of allegiance to Adolf Hitler. Their officers wore former regular Greek Army uniforms, with modified Greek national insignia, lacking the Greek Royal Crown.

Initially, the establishment of a security battalion was 300 NCOs and riflemen, led by 20 (ex-regular Greek Army) officers. Security battalions doubled in size as the National Resistance persisted, with German liaison officers attached to them. Security battalion members were recruited from a cross-section of Greek society: while many of them were draftees, it was conservatives, extreme right-wingers, socially marginalized elements and criminals that were over-represented in their ranks. Plans to establish security battalions in Macedonia and other parts of occupied Greece were scrapped, meaning that their main theatres of operation were Athens, the eastern part of central Greece and the Peloponnese. Their core mission, which they continued to perform into the final days of the German occupation, was the fight against guerrilla bands, in support of the German forces, and the enforcement of punitive measures in the context of anti-partisan operations. In performing their mission, their members committed atrocities and numerous criminal acts against civilians.

The security battalions were complemented by some 22 volunteer battalions, spread across Greece, of which the first one, 'Leonidas' (later, 'Laconia'), was formed in Sparta in September 1943. Volunteer battalions were established in Attica, Euboea, Central Greece, the Peloponnese, Crete, the Ionian Sea islands and Macedonia, where they operated under Schimana's overall command. These were variously termed *Freiwillige-Bataillone*, *Freiwillige-Polizei-Bataillone* or *Freiwillige-Polizei-Halb-Bataillone*, and they were typically identified by reference to their respective city/area of operations, e.g. Freiwillige-Polizei-Bataillon 'Saloniki', or by a combination of Latin numerals and place identifiers, e.g. Freiwillige-Bataillon VI (Kozani). According to an August 1944 ELAS GHQ report, the combined forces of armed collaborationist units totalled about 15,000 men, but other sources estimated their number as well over 20,000 men.

A variety of other collaborationist militias operated in the north of Greece (Macedonia, Thrace and Epirus), where the authority of the Greek puppet government was limited. Their distinguishing features were their leader-centric nature, their semi-official status and their greater degree of autonomy compared to the security and volunteer battalions in southern Greece. One of the most prominent of these militias was EES, the brainchild of a certain Kyriakos Papadopoulos. Locally known by his Turkish nickname of 'Kısa Bacak' (i.e. 'Short Leg'), Papadopoulos was a Turkophone Pontic Greek and veteran partisan leader with guerrilla experience against the Turks between 1914 and 1922. After the fall of Greece, Papadopoulos established a militia, which he armed with weapons recovered from the crumbling Greek Army.

Politically conservative and anti-Communist, Papadopoulos rejected ELAS's repeated invitations to join their ranks. Frustrated in their attempts to win him over, ELAS declared war against his band in the spring of 1943. Augmented by former members of other Resistance bands, which ELAS had dispersed – including EKKA and YBE/PAO – his militia of civilian village guards was gradually driven into the arms of the Germans who, in exchange for weapons and support, used EES men as auxiliaries in their fight against Communist resistance. As EES commander-in-chief, Papadopoulos moved his headquarters from the village of Koukos (Pieria) to Thessaloniki in August 1944, from where he directed his militia's operations until his death, on 4 November 1944, in the battle of Kilkis, in which ELAS definitively vanquished what remained of the anti-Communist collaborationist militias of northern Greece.

THE RECKONING

Measured in terms of the number of Axis troop losses it inflicted and the tying down of enemy troops it entailed, Greece's World War II partisan movement was a success, especially considering the relatively limited Allied investment in human capital and *matériel* in support of the Greek resistance. At the peak of its strength, in late 1944, the Allied Military Mission fielded no more than 400 men.

Starting with the enemy casualty metric, the consensus is that guerrilla action exacted a toll of up to 15,000 killed, 8,000 wounded and between 3,000 and 5,000 prisoners for all the occupation forces put together (without counting those – mostly Italian troops – who surrendered voluntarily to the *andartes*). Thus, for every seven German troops that served in Greece, one had become a casualty by the time of the end of the occupation (the ratio was lower for Germany's Italian and Bulgarian allies). No reliable figures are available on the casualties suffered by the *andartes*, but it is fair to assume that these were comparable, both

in absolute terms and as a ratio, to those of the occupation armies. What is noteworthy in the above estimates is the great preponderance of dead to wounded, testifying to the ferocity of guerrilla warfare in Greece, and to the 'no prisoners' policy pursued by all sides. That said, casualties among Greece's civilian population dwarfed those suffered by the resistance and occupation forces alike between May 1941 and October 1944: an estimated 500,000 civilians had perished by the end of the occupation, of whom about 270,000 died of famine, a staggering 70,000 became victims of reprisals and nearly 50,000, mostly Greek Jews, were deported and exterminated in the German death camps. In terms of the share of its pre-war population that became a fatality during World War II, Greece was only surpassed by Poland, the Soviet Union and Germany.

Turning to the tie-down metric, the existence of a vigorous guerrilla movement in the mountains of Greece was to prove highly disruptive to the German war effort, especially around the time of the preparation and conduct of the Allied landings in Sicily. At the height of World War II, no fewer than 27 Axis divisions were tied down in Greece. The intensification of partisan warfare, as of early 1943, necessitated the involvement of at least two front-line German divisions, which, if available for service in Italy, would, as minimum, have decelerated the pace of the Allies' march to Rome, rendering it more costly in Allied personnel and *matériel*.

Where Greek resistance scored even higher was in terms of its value at interdicting enemy lines of communication. The sabotage operation against the Gorgopotamos River railway bridge cut off the flow of supplies to the Deutsches Afrikakorps for nearly six weeks (39 days), helping to tip the scales of the war in North Africa in the Allies' favour. Similarly, the occupation forces' constant struggle to keep open the few west–east and north–south communications axes in mainland Greece caused them considerable attrition, reinforced their insecurity, and solidified their conviction that, at least in that small corner of Europe, they were, in equal measure, despised and unwanted by the great majority of the population.

FURTHER READING

Condit, D.M. (1961). *Case Study in Guerrilla War: Greece During World War II*. Washington, DC: United States Army Special Operations Command.

Department of the Army (1954). *German Anti-guerrilla Operations in the Balkans (1941–1944)*. Pamphlet No. 20-243. Washington, DC: Department of the Army.

Fricke, G. (1967). 'Das Unternehmen des XXII. Gebirgsarmeekorps Gegen die Inseln Kefalonia und Korfu im Rahmen des Falles 'Achse' September 1943', *Militärgeschichtliche Zeitschrift* 1: 31–58.

Kalogrias, V. (2015). 'Collaborationism and Red Terror in Greek Macedonia, 1943–1944', *Qualestoria* 2: 99–118.

Kalogrias, V. (2008). Draža Mihailović – Napoleon Zervas: A comparative analysis of Resistance and Collaboration in Serbia and Greece (1941–1944). Available at https://www.imxa.gr/files/bsfiles/50/9.Kalogrias-web.pdf (accessed 22 April 2024).

Kazamias, G.A. (1999). 'The usual Bulgarian Stratagems: The Big Three and the End of the Bulgarian Occupation of Greek Eastern Macedonia and Thrace', *European History Quarterly* 29(3): 323–47.

Kotzageorgi, X. & Kazamias, G.A. (1994). 'The Bulgarian Occupation of the Prefecture of Drama (1941–1944) and its Consequences on the Greek Population', *Balkan Studies* 35(1): 81–112.

Melson, C.D. (2011). 'German Counterinsurgency Revisited', *Journal of Military and Strategic Studies* 14(1): 1–33.

Pappas, N.C.J. (2018). 'Brigands and Brigadiers: The Problem of Banditry and the Military in Nineteenth-Century Greece', *Athens Journal of History* 4(3): 175–96.

Petrov, B. (2008). 'The Activities of General Tsolakoglou to retain the Territorial Integrity of Occupied Greece', *Études Balkaniques* 2008/1: 61–80.

Richter, H. (1989). 'General Lanz, Napoleon Zervas und die britischen Verbindungsoffiziere', *Militärgeschichtliche Zeitschrift* 45(1): 111–38.

Shrader S.S. (2008). 'British Military Mission (BMM) to Greece, 1942–1944'. Fort Leavenworth, KS: School of Advanced Military Studies, US Army Command and General Staff College. Available at https://apps.dtic.mil/sti/tr/pdf/ADA506219.pdf (accessed 22 April 2024).

Tsoutsoumpis, S. (2016). *A History of the Greek Resistance in the Second World War: The People's Armies*. Manchester: Manchester University Press.

Wittmer, L.A. (2019). 'SOF in Large-Scale Combat Operations: An Operational Level Analysis of the British SOE in Crete and Greece during World War II'. Fort Leavenworth, KS: School of Advanced Military Studies, US Army Command and General Staff College.

Zeleppos, I. (2021). 'Collaboration in Greece 1941–1944', in M. Bitunjac & J.H. Schoeps, eds, *Complicated Complicity – European Collaboration with Nazi Germany during World War II*, Berlin: De Gruyter: pp. 213–28.

PLATE COMMENTARIES

A: RESISTANCE LEADERS
A1: Protokapetánios Aris Velouchiòtis, ELAS GHQ, Lamia, October 1944
Except for his fur *kalpak* and British Army leather jerkin, Arch-Captain Velouchiòtis, aged 39 in 1944, is portrayed here wearing the khaki wool uniform of a pre-war regular Greek Army officer, stripped of rank insignia or branch identifiers. His breeches are tucked into black leather cavalry boots – Velouchiòtis and his retinue of bodyguards travelled by horse, with cavalry accoutrements being an indispensable part of their attire – while the decorative dagger hanging from his waist belt is reminiscent of that of military academy cadets.

A2: Antistrátigos Stefanos Saráfis, Caserta, Naples, September 1944
ELAS's overall military commander is shown here in the service uniform of a lieutenant-general, which he donned at the time of the negotiations that led to the signing of the Caserta Agreement. His uniform is, essentially, that of a pre-war regular Greek Army general officer except for a six-pointed, oversize silver-thread-embroidered star on each of his tunic's shoulder straps; these were a rank distinction unique to Saráfis, whose pre-war Greek Army rank was that of an infantry colonel. His collar insignia, in the form of a gold-thread-embroidered oak leaf set against a red tab, is that worn to this day by regular Greek Army general officers. His forage cap, which sports an embroidered white-and-blue stylized flaming grenade, with the letters 'ELAS' at its base, was on display, at the time of publication, at the Athens War Museum.

A3: Syntagmatàrchis Napoleon Zervas, Derviziani, November 1942
The overall military commander of EDES wears a pre-war regular Greek Army uniform, stripped of rank insignia or branch identifiers. The buttons that fasten his tunic are not the standard-issue, convex-shaped, gold-coloured metal buttons bearing the Greek coat of arms but instead plain plastic, brown-coloured substitutes, in a show of defiance to the Monarchy, which Colonel Zervas had originally opposed as guerrilla leader (but was to later embrace, for reasons of political convenience). His Sam Browne belt and leather pistol holster were also standard issue for Greek Army officers of the period.

B: RESISTANCE FORCES (1)
B1: *Dioikitìs tagmatos*, ELAS, Amfissa, June 1944
This smartly dressed senior ELAS officer is depicted in the late stages of the National Resistance. His outfit is reminiscent, in its cut, of the service uniform worn by Greek Army officers until Greece's capitulation to the Axis. It would have been made of British-supplied cloth, as former Greek Army uniform stocks had been largely depleted by this stage of World War II. He wears leather riding boots and a Sam Browne belt for his service weapon (most likely, a British-supplied revolver), items indicative of his officer status. His

rank of battalion commander is denoted by the single, six-pointed, gold-coloured metal star pinned on each of his tunic's epaulettes, and on the right-hand side of his British Army-inspired forage cap.

B2: *Mavroskoufis*, ELAS, Viniani, October 1943
Formed in April 1943, the *Mavroskoufides* ('Black Hoods'), named after their characteristic black fur *kalpaks*, were a mounted squadron of about 50 hand-picked men, some of them former bandits and outlaws, who served as the personal guards of Aris Velouchiòtis. The forbidding-looking *Mavroskoufis* portrayed here carries a plentiful supply of ammunition in leather cartridge belts, as well as a decorated waist knife, reminiscent of those carried at the time of the Greek War of Independence.

B3: *Andartissa*, 34th Parnassus Regiment, ELAS, Dervenochoria, October 1943
This artwork depicts a female partisan as she would have appeared in late 1943, in the mountains of central Greece. She is armed with a 7.92mm Kar 98k rifle, taken from a dead German soldier. By this stage of the war, British supplies had begun to give ELAS guerrillas a more uniform, military

Stéfanos Saráfis, military commander of ELAS, poses next to its *protokapetánios*, Aris Velouchiòtis. Their close cooperation helped to propel ELAS to the front rank of Greece's wartime resistance movement. During the early stages of the Greek Civil War, Velouchiòtis was ambushed and died in the Agrafa Mountains on 15 June 1945, with the circumstances of his death remaining the subject of controversy to this day. Saráfis survived World War II and the Greek Civil War, went into politics and died in a collision with a car in a suburb of Athens, on 31 May 1957. Standing between the two men is one of the bodyguards of Velouchiòtis (see Plate B2), possibly Leon Tzavellas, the *nom de guerre* of Ioannis Aggeletos. (Athens War Museum)

appearance, with the *andartissa* portrayed here turned out in British Army-supplied battledress, a British Army service coat and leather laced ankle boots.

C: RESISTANCE FORCES (2)
C1: *Dioikitìs tagmatos*, Athens Division, ELAS, October 1944
This ELAS battalion commander is from the Asia Minor refugee-dominated neighbourhoods of east Athens, underneath Mount Ymittos. He is turned out in a mix of locally made and 'liberated' uniform items, including former Greek Army or locally made legwear; German jackboots; a German open-collared tropical tunic, complete with its distinctive stipple-pattern buttons; and a Greek Army-style forage cap. His rank is denoted by the single, six-pointed, gold-thread-embroidered star stitched to his tunic's epaulettes. He is armed with a .32 FN/Browning 1900 semi-automatic pistol and has a binocular case (not visible here) slung around his back.

C2: *Aetópoulo*, ELAS, Paramythia, April 1944
Based on a characteristic period photograph, this child partisan is depicted as he would have appeared in the closing stages of the Greek resistance. He is turned out in British-supplied battledress, adjusted to his diminutive proportions, and is armed with a 6.5mm Mannlicher-Carcano M1891 cavalry carbine, well suited, due to its light weight, to the capabilities of child soldiers. He carries a plentiful supply of ammunition in locally sourced leather bandoliers and belts, and his headdress is a forage cap devoid of insignia; some ELAS guerrillas wore homemade metal or cloth badges on their headgear. Children aged 9–14 were eligible for service in the ranks of ELAS, as so-called *Aétopoula* ('Eagle-chicks'), and many of them volunteered for service, especially as of 1944, as ELAS expanded.

C3: *Andartis*, 24th Regiment, EDES, Splantza, October 1943
This typical EDES partisan is depicted as he would have appeared in Epirus, the EDES stronghold. Except for his characteristic former regular Greek Army forage cap, his double-pin leather waist belt and his puttees, most of his other uniform items are British-supplied, down to his double-breasted British Army cold-weather officers' overcoat (so-called 'Officers' Warm'). He is armed with a holstered revolver, and with a venerable Gras Mle 1874 bolt-action artillery musketoon, of regular Greek Army pedigree, with spare ammunition carried in crossed leather bandoliers.

D: RESISTANCE FORCES (3)
D1: SOE liaison officer, Roumeli, May 1943
A BLO, as he would have appeared in the mountains of central Greece in 1943, after the successful Gorgopotamos River railway bridge sabotage operation had been transformed into an ongoing mission to help organize and steer resistance against the Axis occupiers. He is turned out in a 'Battledress, Serge' uniform (often referred to as '1937 Pattern'), consisting of a bloused tunic featuring a five-button fly front, pleated pockets with concealed buttons and an unlined collar; matching trousers featuring a large map-pocket on the front of the left leg with a concealed button and a small, single pleat dressing pocket on the front of the right hip; and canvas anklets. He also sports a waistcoat-style, collarless, sleeveless and pocketless tan leather single-breasted jerkin, fastened with four plastic buttons. The jerkin is lined in khaki 'Battledress' serge material, for added

protection against the cold. He is armed with a service revolver, slung from a canvas belt.

D2: *Dioikitis tagmatos*, 40th Regiment, EDES, Derviziani, April 1943

Period photographs show EDES commanders turned out in a combination of uniform items of Greek, British and Axis origin. This battalion commander is closely based on a period photograph of Gheorghios Agoros (see page 17). He wears an *Evzoni*-type low fez, with the hand-embroidered Greek letters 'EΔES' and 'EOE' (for 'Greek National Bands') on his forage cap, with a stylized Greek cross framed within the letter 'O'; a battledress blouse; pre-war regular Greek Army breeches; and cleated jackboots. He is armed with a holstered revolver, slung from his hip, for which he carries ammunition both in a waist belt and in a locally made leather bandolier, and a 6.5mm Mannlicher-Schönauer M1903/14 rifle, from former regular Greek Army stocks. The majority of EDES commanders were former regular Greek Army officers, some with pro- and others with anti-Monarchist political leanings, but with a common language traceable to their formal military training, which, at least in the earlier stages of the National Resistance, gave EDES units a certain tactical superiority over rival guerrilla bands.

D3: *Andartis*, 2nd Regiment, ELAS, Thebes, November 1944

An ELAS guerrilla, as he would have appeared in Roumeli, around the closing stages of the Axis occupation. His headdress is a modified Greek Army-issue forage cap, with no visible affiliation badges, his personal weapon is a British-supplied Thompson M1928 blowback SMG (a prized possession in the mountains of Greece), and the object he is holding on to in his left hand is a make-shift water-canteen, carved out of a pumpkin, an example of which is on display at the Helioupolis National Resistance Museum (Athens).

E: AXIS OCCUPATION FORCES (1)

E1: *Küstenjäger*, Küstenjäger-Abteilung 'Brandenburg', Rhodes, July 1943

The coastal raider shown here – soon to go into action against the British and the Italians in Leros – is turned out in warm-weather garb, consisting of shorts, a single-breasted, open-collar M40 *Feldbluse*, an M43 *Einheitsfeldmütze* and short tropical boots. The *Feldbluse*, which was worn over a lightweight cotton service shirt, fastens with five stipple-pattern buttons, and features sewn double *Litzen* collar patches, the *Heeresadler* on the right breast, detachable tropical-pattern shoulder straps with *Waffenfarbe* piping, pleated breast pockets with squared button flaps, bellows skirt pockets with squared button flaps, concealed button cuffs, a rear vent and two belt hooks fitted to the rear waistband. The veteran *Brandenburgers* were to prove their mettle in the autumn of 1943 when, despite their numerical disadvantage, they prevailed against the reticent Italian garrisons of the Dodecanese islands and their British allies, in successful amphibious operations in Kos (Operation *Eisbär*) and Leros (Operation *Leopard*).

E2: *Gefreiter*, Jäger-Regiment 724, Agrinio, June 1943

The 104. Jäger-Division was posted to western Greece in June 1943, and remained there until its withdrawal to Yugoslavia, where it fought against Tito's Partisans. The corporal portrayed here wears a standard-issue M43 *Feldbluse*: on the upper right sleeve is the *Jäger* badge, also

Four identified ELAS *andartes* (from left to right, Louis Kohen, Gheorgios Katsigiannis, Nikos Dimitriou and David Brudo), all members of the 2nd Parnassus Regiment, triumphantly enter the town of Thiva in October 1944, shortly after the German withdrawal. (© Photographic Archive – Jewish Museum of Greece)

worn on the *Einheitsfeldmütze*, in the form of a white-metal pin. His tapered M43 trousers are tucked into his cleated *Bergschuhe* (mountaineering boots). He carries a Tellermine 42 anti-tank mine, with an explosive charge of 5.5kg of Amatol. Although these were not suitable as anti-personnel weapons (their activation required the application of a weight of at least 210kg), they could, if strung together and detonated remotely, be used as demolition charges, to blow up fortified positions, tree-trunks and smaller bridges, helping to interdict the *andartes'* escape routes and to flush them out of their dugouts during anti-partisan operations.

E3: *SS-Sturmmann*, SS-Polizei-Panzergrenadier-Regiment 7, Larissa, June 1944

Waffen-SS units active in south-eastern Europe (but also in Ukraine and the Caucasus) were turned out in tropical uniforms, often modelled after Italian uniform items. The *SS-Sturmmann* shown here wears a lightweight, Italian-style *Sahariana* shirt with a tropical M43 *Einheitsfeldmütze*. His Luftwaffe-inspired baggy trousers, bloused over half-canvas/half-leather lace-up boots, were also worn by Heer and Waffen-SS units operating in the warmer climates of south-eastern Europe and the Mediterranean. The *SS-Sturmmann* is only recognizable as a member of the Waffen-SS by the *Totenkopf* (death's head) skull-and-bones symbol on his peaked cap and by the conspicuous absence of the *Wehrmachtsadler* eagle-shaped national emblem over the right breast pocket. On 5 April 1944, members of SS-Polizei-Panzergrenadier-Regiment 7 murdered some 270 of the inhabitants of the village of Klisoura (western Macedonia) in reprisals for the death of two of their comrades in the hands of the *andartes*.

F: AXIS OCCUPATION FORCES (2)

F1: *Caporale*, 13° Reggimento di fanteria 'Pinerolo', Kastoria, November 1942

A corporal in the typical grey-green uniform of Italy's army, as he would have appeared on any of the Continental fronts on which Italy fought until its surrender in September 1943. He wears the M40 single-breasted grey-green *giubba*, featuring an integral belt, and matching trousers, and has standard-issue grey-green leather webbing, from which a frogged knife-bayonet is suspended. His headgear is the M33/34 nickel-steel helmet, varnished in dull grey-green, and his weapon is the 6.5mm Mannlicher-Carcano M1891 rifle – one of the most outdated standard-issue rifles fielded by any of the armed forces that participated in World War II.

F2: *SS-Unterscharführer*, SS-Pionier-Bataillon 4, Kozani, July 1944

The 4. SS-Polizei-Panzergrenadier-Division, the home formation of this soldier, transferred to Greece from France, where it was rebuilt in early 1943, following its involvement in heavy combat action on the Eastern Front. While in Greece, it was involved in intense anti-partisan action, mostly against ELAS units. The NCO depicted here wears an Italian-style *Sahariana* jacket over a lightweight shirt, and matching baggy tropical trousers. He is protected against the Greek sun by a second-pattern (i.e. felt as opposed to canvas-covered)

Four German servicemen (including two ranking as *Gefreiter* and one *Obergefreiter*) pose for the camera before the Royal Palace in Athens (the present-day Parliament Building). Three of them are wearing standard Luftwaffe service and walking-out uniforms. The 'odd man out' (standing second from the left) wears what looks like a standard Luftwaffe tropical uniform, and what appear to be *Fallschirmjäger* (paratroopers) front-laced jump boots; his belt buckle is unmistakably that of the Luftwaffe, but his rank is impossible to identify in this photograph (on tropical uniforms, this was solely displayed on the shoulder straps, which are not visible here). (Author's Collection)

Tropenhelm (pith helmet), which was issued, in limited numbers, for non-front-line use, to SS personnel stationed in North Africa, Italy, Greece and the Caucasus, mostly without insignia. His rank is indicated on his collar tabs, with the right-side tab bearing dual, machine-embroidered runes and the left-side tab featuring a single silvered pip, and on his shoulder straps, trimmed with branch-colour piping and bordered by wire tresses. Stitched onto his upper left sleeve is a Waffen-SS-style eagle and onto his lower left arm a cuff title consisting of a black rayon base, trimmed along both edges with silver aluminium wire tresses, and bearing the machine-embroidered inscription of 'SS-POLIZEI-DIVISION'. His decorations include the *Eisernes Kreuz 2. Klasse* (Iron Cross Second Class), the *Nahkampfspange in Bronze* (Close Combat Clasp in Bronze) and the *Verwundetenabzeichen in Schwarz* (Wound Badge in Black). He is armed with a holstered Walther P 38 pistol, the standard sidearm for officers, NCOs and machine-gun crews serving with the Heer, the Luftwaffe, the Kriegsmarine and the Waffen-SS.

F3: *Carabiniere*, VI Battaglione Carabinieri Reali, Messolonghi, March 1943

The Carabinieri Reali, Italy's Gendarmerie-type militarized police force, supported the Regio Esercito in its occupation and security tasks, with units of Carabinieri attached to most of the Army's major occupation formations throughout Greece during 1941–43. The *Carabiniere* portrayed here wears the characteristic *Carabinieri lucerne* (tricorne), with a *grigio-verde* (grey-green) cover, adorned with an embroidered stylized flaming grenade bearing the letters 'VE' (for Vittorio Emmanuelle, the King of Italy), but without the full-dress, red-over-blue plume; an M40 single-breasted grey-green *giubba* (tunic) – four-button light beige *Sahariana* summer tunics were worn, instead, during the warmer months – complete with the silver-coloured laced *Carabinieri mostrine* (insignia), featuring the Italian armed forces' five-pointed star; and grey-green pantaloons. His brown leather bandolier (at the lower end of which a pistol holster is suspended), which was standard issue for Italian mounted and armoured troops during World War II, was also worn by the Carabinieri. His main weapon is the ubiquitous Mannlicher-Carcano M1891 cavalry carbine.

G: BULGARIAN OCCUPATION FORCES

G1: *Podpolkovnik*, 7th Infantry Division, Thessaloniki, March 1943

Following the Bulgarian Army's reorganization in 1936, the design of the uniforms worn by its men underwent considerable changes, with officers' uniforms borrowing German Army uniform-inspired elements. Differences remained, however, in terms of colour (which fluctuated between olive drab and khaki), the tunics' shoulder boards (which remained styled after those of the Imperial Russian Army), and the three-pointed shape of the tunic's breast and side pocket flaps (styled after those of the Austro-Hungarian Army, with deeply scalloped pocket flaps that formed long points at their ends). The single-breasted tunic's stand-and-fall collars featured German-style double *Litzen* for ranks below that of general, and the service-dress breeches and riding boots of Bulgarian Army officers were very similar to those worn by their German Army counterparts. The lieutenant-colonel portrayed here wears the winter version of the 1936-pattern service uniform, made of heavy wool, and carries a map case (concealing his holstered service pistol, suspended over the right hip from his Sam Browne-style belt). His headdress is similar in style to the contemporary Italian *bustina* forage cap and features a metal shield with the Bulgarian tricolour on its right-hand side, and a crowned lion rampant badge on its front.

G2: *Rednik*, 16th Infantry Division, Xanthi, October 1942

The 1936 reforms did not leave rank-and-file Bulgarian Army uniforms unaffected, even if their impact was less radical than in the case of officers' uniforms. The reservist private portrayed here is turned out in the standard 'tobacco brown' woollen winter service uniform, with red (infantry) collar patches and matching (pre-war) shoulder straps. He also wears the M1936 steel helmet (distinguishable from the M1938 helmet by its characteristic frontal crest), and standard-issue infantry leather equipment. He is armed with an 8mm Steyr-Mannlicher M1895/1934 rifle, in service in the Bulgarian Army from 1935. Instead of the more common jackboots, he wears ankle boots with the tapered ends of his woollen trousers constrained by canvas gaiters, secured in place by two buttons.

G3: *Polkovnik*, 11th Infantry Division, Komotini (Gjumjurdschina), June 1941

Bulgaria owed its independence from Ottoman rule to the intervention by Imperial Russia, which was also the source of the original (and, in some respects, the most lasting) influence on the uniforms of its troops. The Imperial Russian Army pedigree of this colonel's uniform is unmistakable, evinced by his *furashka*-like peaked cap, the oval-shaped national cockade, and the Imperial Russian Army-inspired shoulder boards. His staff-officer status is denoted by his braided aiguillettes and the wide red stripe along the seams of his breeches. His *mundir* (tunic) is the lighter-weight summer variant, in olive-drab wool; white cotton or linen variants of the tunic were also in use during the summer months, and these featured a high standing collar and standard shoulder boards.

H: COLLABORATIONIST FORCES

H1: *Evzon*, 2nd Security Regiment, Patras, May 1944

Rank and file serving with the state-sanctioned security battalions were turned out in the *Evzoni* version of the pre-war beige summer service uniform (although, in period photographs, they present a somewhat dejected and less 'military' appearance compared to their precursors). The *Evzoni* service uniform consisted of a traditional, zouave-style low fez (devoid of the long black tassel typical of pre-war *Evzoni* service dress), a frock-type *doulama* (tunic), gartered woollen stockings and mountaineers' hobnailed *tsarouhia* (shoes). The black woollen pompoms featuring on his shoes were normally removed when in the field (although occupation-period *Evzoni* appear to have worn them regularly). The *Evzon* portrayed here is armed with a Mannlicher-Schönauer M1903/14 rifle, from former regular Greek Army stocks; his equipment is that of the pre-war regular Greek Army, and his fez displays no national cockade.

H2: *Ypostràtigos*, 1st Security Regiment, Athens, September 1943

Security battalion officers were mostly former regular Greek Army officers re-activated to command the state-sanctioned security battalions. Unsurprisingly, officers serving with those units were turned out in M1938 uniforms (here, the No. 4 Service Dress uniform worn by a major-general) as worn by regular Greek Army officers until the outbreak of World War II. This consisted of a 'French-style' officers' tunic, matching breeches, brown leather riding boots and a British Army-style

Two grim-looking EDES guerrillas pose for the camera, somewhere in the mountains of Greece, during the National Resistance. They both wear battledress, as was commonplace for the members of many Allied-supported guerrilla bands in Greece from 1943 onwards. The man on the left wears the US-manufactured War Aid battledress, while the man on the right wears the original Serge (or Pattern 1937) version. The medal ribbon visible above each left breast pocket of the blouse cannot be identified. (Athens War Museum)

peaked cap with a leather visor. The occupation-period 'Greek State' was a peculiar type of anti-Monarchist republic, subservient to its Axis masters. As a result, the one material respect in which the uniforms worn by the security battalion officers differed from those of the pre-war regular Greek Army was the absence of the Greek Royal Crown from the embroidered white-and-blue round-shaped national cockade that adorned their peaked caps, as well as from the shoulder straps of higher-ranking officers.

H3: Militiaman, *Lòchos Asfaleias*, EES, Kozani, March 1944

EES militiamen were, essentially, armed village guards, whose task was to protect their area of responsibility from ELAS bands' incursions. They were, therefore, dressed in civilian garb, apart from the occasional identifying badge. The militiaman depicted here is based on a period photograph; he wears a makeshift white cloth armband, featuring a rendition of the Swastika, next to a stylized version of the Greek flag and what looks like the Latin letter 'V'. He is armed with a Mannlicher-Schönauer M1903/14 rifle, and also carries a Czech 7.92mm ZB-26 light machine gun, supplied by the Germans.

INDEX

References to illustration captions are shown in **bold**. Plates are shown with page and caption locators in brackets.